Spiritual Warrior Woman: Pray

Dr. Angela Ruark
&
The Sisterhood of Prayer Warriors

STAND FIRM
RESOURCES

Spiritual Warrior Woman: Pray

Copyright © 2020 by Angela Ruark

Published by Stand Firm Books www.standfirmministries.com

General Editor: Rita Halter Thomas with Stand Firm Books
Compilation Editor: Dr. Angela Ruark

Spiritual Warrior Woman Series vol. 1
Second Printing

ISBN: 978-0-578-70192-9

"...Pray without ceasing..." 1 Thessalonians 5:17

Table of Contents

Part 1

Preparing Your Weapons

Part 2

Wielding Your Weapons

𝔓𝔞𝔯𝔱 3

The Sisterhood of Prayer Warriors

Acknowledgments

I would like to give special thanks to Jake McCandless, founder and executive director of Stand Firm Ministries and creator of the Spiritual Warrior Devotional Series. It is an honor to write the Spiritual Warrior Woman devotionals and be part of the Stand Firm team. Thank you for all you do and for your support for this project.

Rita Halter Thomas, what a triple blessing it has been to work with you on this book. Not only did I end up with a wonderful editor and contributing writer, but I also gained a friend. Thank you for your encouragement and expertise. I look forward to future projects with you!

To all the contributing writers—let me say to each one of you—that I am truly grateful to know you and that you are part of this book. I admire each of you and pray that you all continue to be the mighty spiritual warrior women you are. Thank you for taking time to share your stories.

My family and friends, thank you for hanging in there with me as I worked on this project. Thank you for understanding the long hours. Your encouragement kept me going.

Last but not least, I would like to thank my husband, Bill. You know that I could not have done this without you. Thank you for keeping me going, listening to me for hours on end, and giving me great feedback and encouragement. God blesses me over and over with you.

Dedication

This book is lovingly dedicated to my mom, Sandra Baggett Dietrich, who gained her eternal victory just before this book was completed. I will see you on the other side.

Introduction

I am so glad you have chosen to spend your valuable time reading *Spiritual Warrior Woman: Pray*. My prayer is that you will be inspired, encouraged, and challenged to grow closer to Jesus and deepen your walk with Him through reading this book. I hope this devotional will be something you can reference again and again as you follow Jesus.

When Jake McCandless, the founder of Stand Firm Ministries, first described the idea of the Spiritual Warrior devotionals, I immediately felt called to be part. I am honored that I have had the privilege and blessing of writing this first installment of the women's series. As I began writing, God made it clear to me that not only were there incredible examples of spiritual warrior women in the Bible, but there were also some incredible spiritual warrior women I personally knew!

We began contacting them, asking them to share their stories and testimonies—of going through the fire—and emerging with a stronger faith than ever before. In writing this book, I feel like I became the curator of a wonderful collection of God's works of art in the lives of women from the past and the present.

Within these pages, you will discover a field manual of sorts to help prepare and strengthen you for the spiritual battles we face every day (Ephesians 6:12). In Part I, Preparing Your Weapons, you'll find examples of women from the Bible that discuss important principles of prayer and how they apply to our lives. Part II, Wielding Your Weapons, provides powerful testimonies of modern-day spiritual warrior women as they live out these principles in their own lives. You'll also find Going Deeper sections from notable Christian women authors who take a more in-depth look at principles of prayer. Each daily devotion contains a journal entry and prompt to help you reflect over important points from the reading. In Part III, The Sisterhood of Prayer Warriors, you'll be able to meet each contributing author and find out more about them.

I am excited for you to discover what lies ahead. Whether you are working hard to raise your children, care for your husband, facing a devastating diagnosis, dealing with grief, pain, or just simply trying to make it through another day, you are not alone in your fight. Let these stories of real women from the past and present inspire and encourage you, that in Jesus, our victory is assured.

Jesus said in John 16:33, "In the world you will have tribulation, but take heart, I have overcome the world." Let us remember His words as we go to war for our families, ourselves, and for the salvation of others. The time is now—to get on our knees and fight!

In His Service,

Dr. Angela Ruark

"For you have armed me with strength for the battle..."
Psalms 18:39

Part 1

Preparing Your Weapons

Chapter 1

Trust: Deborah

恶

"Has not the Lord gone out before you?" Judges 4:14

Deborah was a judge and prophetess of Israel. When we are first introduced to her in the Book of Judges, she had been judging Israel for some time. Judges 4:1 says the children of Israel had done "evil in the sight of the Lord" which led to their severe oppression under the king of Canaan. This oppression had been going on for twenty years and caused the children of Israel to call out to the Lord for help. The Bible tells us that Deborah "would sit under the palm tree of Deborah between Ramah and Bethel in the mountains of Ephraim...and the children of Israel came up to her for judgment" (verse 5). Deborah's role was to hear from God and instruct the Israelites on what to do.

Imagine for a moment the scene: here is Deborah, sitting under a palm tree, probably on a hillside, surrounded by mountains and valleys. I am sure it was lush and green and beautiful—modern photos let us see how it looks today. After all, this was the land of Canaan, the promised land. Yet, because of Israel's disobedience, they were not the conquerors they were supposed to be. Then we read that Deborah sent for the commander of the armies of Israel. Her message to him in verse six implies some inaction on his part. When he arrives, she begins with, "Has not the Lord commanded..." As we continue reading, we learn that the military leader refused to attack as God had commanded, even though there was a promise of victory given with the command. The leader tells Deborah the only way he would go was if she went with him. And she did. Scripture says they led ten thousand men.

So here is Deborah, a prophetess, a wife, a songwriter, leading the armies of Israel. She was a woman who trusted God. And when it was time to engage the enemy, she posed the question, "Has not the Lord gone out before you?" This simple question implies so much. She is asking the commander of the armies of Israel: Didn't God tell you to do something? Didn't He promise He would be with you and give you victory? What are you waiting for? Go!

There is solid foundation for Deborah to ask this question the way she did. As a judge of the children of Israel, she would have spent much time praying, hearing from the Lord, trusting what He said to be true, and witnessing Him keep His promises. To send tens of thousands of soldiers into battle with a promise of victory takes complete faith in what God says. Deborah had absolute trust in God and did not limit Him in any way. She knew beyond a doubt that if the Lord had gone before them, then victory was assured.

In our daily lives, we have a tendency to put limits on God. In spite of all the incredible miracles we know He has done, we somehow convince ourselves that whatever we are facing is just too hard for God, that it isn't important, or maybe He just won't answer. Why do we do this when the Bible is so clear about how much He desires to help us? Isaiah 41:10 reminds us: "Fear not, for I am with you; Be not dismayed, for I am your God. I will strengthen you, Yes, I will help you, I will uphold you with My righteous right hand."

If we are to truly take our place as spiritual warrior women, we need to put our faith where our mouth is when it comes to trusting God. This means that if we say we trust Him, then we REALLY need to do just that—in every area of our lives and without limits. As women, we are detail-oriented, and we tend to worry over those details. How much precious time is lost by our fretting? Wouldn't it make our lives so much easier if we put everything in God's hands? And then left it there?

Take a look at Philippians 4:6-7: "Be anxious for nothing, but in everything by prayer and supplication, with thanksgiving, let your requests be made known to God; and the peace of God which surpasses all understanding, will guard your hearts and minds through Christ Jesus."

It may seem next to impossible to be anxious for nothing right now in your life. But read again what it says in Philippians. The remedy for all the anxiety, stress, and worry is written right there—"but in EVERYTHING [what we worry over—emphasis mine] by prayer and supplication [what we are supposed to do], with thanksgiving [how we ask], let your requests be made known unto God [we ask our Abba Father]." Then the rest of the verse is a beautiful promise full of comfort. God tells us that if we put everything in His hands, we will have peace in the midst of trials [because that definitely surpasses understanding] and He will help us through everyday life, whatever comes our way, and we will keep our sanity in the process.

Consider this further thought: a warrior cannot go into battle doubting or with a bunch of baggage. If victory is the goal, then there is only room for weapons. There is no reason to put limits on God to guide us and to see us through every situation. We can completely trust Him the way Deborah did. Let us learn from her example and ask ourselves, "Has not the Lord gone out before you?"

Dear God, thank You that You are faithful and strong when I am weak. Please help me to not limit You in any way in my life. Help me to put everything in Your hands and trust You completely. In Jesus' Name, Amen.

Areas of My Life Where the Lord Has Gone Out Before Me:

_____

_____

_____

_____

Chapter 2

Confidence: The Daughters of Zelophehad

"Then came the daughters of Zelophehad...And they stood before Moses, before Eleazar the priest, and before the leaders and all the congregation..." Numbers 27:1-2

In the Book of Numbers, we read how Israel came through the plague caused by their disobedience. After the plague, the Lord instructed Moses and Eleazar (a priest and son of Aaron) to conduct a census of everyone able to go to war who was twenty years old and older. The census listed the sons and families of the children of Israel, recording names and inheritances. There is an exception in this list. When we read Numbers 26:33, it says, "Now Zelophehad the son of Hepher had no sons, but daughters; and the names of the daughters of Zelophehad were Mahlah, Noah, Hoglah, Milcah, and Tirza." We don't find out why these are the only women included and named until Chapter 27.

Because of the death of their father, who had no sons, these five sisters were stranded without inheritance. This had devastating implications. Unlike today where they could look for work, the daughters of Zelophehad would have likely been impoverished and without opportunities. They were probably desperate. And it was not just their own lives that concerned them. As we study, we learn their primary concern was that their father's name not be lost from the recorded history of the children of Israel. Being eliminated would have lumped him into the category of those whose blatant disobedience to God brought down the plague. Their father, faithful to God, happened to die a death unrelated to turning away from God. So, these women did something unprecedented that took significant courage. The daughters of Zelophehad stood before Moses and the leaders of the nation and made their case. They laid it out simply, logically, and included their motivation for asking in the first place. Moses took their case to the Lord, who responded with, "The daughters of Zelophehad speak what is right..." (Numbers 27:7) and God granted their request. The five sisters received the inheritance.

This is the kind of confidence we need when we pray. Not worldly, self-confidence, but confidence in the Lord–in who He is and who we are in Him. The daughters of Zelophehad give us an example for understanding who we are as God's children and how we can go "boldly to the throne of grace, that we may obtain mercy and find grace to help in time of need" (Hebrews 4:16).

Without their inheritance, how would the daughters of Zelophehad have survived? Their very lives may have been at stake as well as the good name of their father, who had "died in the wilderness," but had not rebelled against the Lord "in company with Korah" (Numbers 27:3). Not only did the daughters want to preserve their family name among the children of Israel, they wanted to rightly claim what was rightly theirs or else their valuable inheritance would be lost! Such a dire circumstance drove them to go and plead their case.

The daughters of Zelophehad went boldly in their time of need. Verse two says: "And they stood before Moses, before Eleazar the priest, and before the leaders and all the congregation, by the doorway of the tabernacle meeting." This is a big deal here. They did not go meekly in hopes that someone would listen. No! They went right to the top, in front of everyone, and laid out their situation. And you know what happened? They received mercy and grace. God even said that what the daughters spoke was right. Wow! What an honor. To be counted right by God is no small thing. It meant that their thinking was aligned with God's thinking. It also meant their hearts were in the right place too, because 1 Chronicles 28:9 says, "For the Lord searches all hearts and understands all the intent of the thoughts." God even honored them by having their names included in the recorded history.

Spiritual warrior women, we need to ask ourselves, do we know what our inheritance is? Do we know its value? Do we understand all that is at stake? It reminds me of what Jesus said

15

to the Samaritan woman at the well. "If you knew the gift of God, and who it is who says to you, 'Give Me a drink,' you would have asked Him, and He would have given you living water" (John 4:10). The inheritance we have in Jesus is beyond anything we can imagine. It is beyond priceless. In the daughters of Zelophehad, we have an example of women wise enough and desperate enough to boldly ask for what belonged to them. How much more desperate should we be to receive what Jesus offers us? Are we wise enough to ask? Are our hearts in the right place?

The heart and mind of a warrior are loyal to the cause and singular of purpose. To become true spiritual warrior women, our hearts need to be in the right place and so do our thoughts and ideas. We need to ask God to work in us in this way. To create in us clean hearts like it says in Psalms 51:10 and in Romans 12:2: "And do not be conformed to this world, but be transformed by the renewing of your mind, that you may prove what is that good and acceptable and perfect will of God." When we take this step, God will begin to change us so our thoughts and motivations align with His and we can know His will. Our prayers will reflect that, and we can take our place as spiritual warrior women, claiming the promise of 1 John 5:14, "Now this is the confidence that we have in Him, that if we ask anything according to His will, He hears us." We will stand with true confidence like the daughters of Zelophehad, and God will hear our prayers.

Dear God, please renew my mind and purify my heart. Help me to have confidence in You and to know and do Your will. Help

16

me to pray for Your will to be done. Please make my thoughts and the intents of my heart align with Yours in all I do and say. Thank You. In Jesus' Name, Amen.

What I Have Confidence in God for:

_____

_____

_____

_____

_____

_____

_____

_____

_____

Chapter 3

Heart: Esther

❦

"...and the king held out to Esther the golden scepter that was in his hand." Esther 5:2

The Book of Esther does not begin by telling us about Esther, but about her predecessor, Vashti. Scripture says Vashti was "beautiful to behold" (Esther 1:11). But continue reading and you quickly learn that on the inside, she was not so hot. She wasn't loyal. In fact, she was downright rebellious and stubborn. She did not have a heart for her king. Eventually, Vashti received her comeuppance and was no longer the queen.

On the advice of counselors, the king launched a search for a replacement, by basically conducting a kingdom-wide beauty pageant to find his new queen. The Bible tells us that beautiful young virgins from all parts of the kingdom were sent

19

to the king's palace to see which young woman pleased the king. Esther was among them.

Her parents died when she was young, so Esther's uncle Mordecai raised her. The Bible describes her as both lovely and beautiful. These words might seem redundant, but it's more likely they are describing two distinct characteristics. While beautiful obviously indicates Esther was pleasing to the eye (a requirement to be sent to the palace in the first place), the choice of the word lovely implies something about her behavior—about her, beyond how she looked.

Merriam-Webster defines lovely as including harmony, grace, moral, and ideal worth. Esther's inner beauty shone through and made her stand out among all the young women. In other words, what was in her heart showed up on her face and in her behavior, amplifying her outer beauty. God gave Esther favor in this way, but it was for a much higher purpose than winning the king's beauty pageant.

When Esther became queen, the king held a feast in her honor and proclaimed a holiday!

At one time or another in our girlhood, most of us probably dreamed of what it would be like to be a princess, a queen, or in a beauty pageant, but how about a holiday named after you? Such attention could have gone to Esther's head, but it didn't. We have a glimpse of Esther as a young girl, which may help us understand why. In Esther 2:20, we read why she had not yet revealed she was a Jew: "for Esther obeyed the command of Mordecai as when she was brought up by him." She was a dutiful and loyal adopted daughter and grew to be a queen of the same nature.

Then comes important assignment number one. In the second chapter of Esther, Mordecai overheard a plot against the king's life. He sent word to Esther, who informed the king. But I want to point out that Esther did not take the glory for herself. Instead, she informed the king in Mordecai's name, not her own! This is further evidence of the loyal heart of Esther. When the investigation revealed that Esther's information was correct, the king's life was saved, and the would-be assassins hung. The details of the entire story were then recorded in the king's history book. Surely, this earned Esther some serious queen points! But I do think it was a precursor to the real test Esther later faced. A test of loyalty—a test of heart. This test required Esther to put her life on the line to save her people.

The king promoted a man named Haman to a very high position in his kingdom—one that demanded homage (by king's decree) from all the servants within the king's gate. Everyone paid Haman homage except for Mordecai. Mordecai's heart was true to God and he refused to bow. This incensed Haman, who launched a plot to kill all of Mordecai's people, the Jews.

Esther's servants told her of Mordecai mourning in sackcloth and ashes. She inquired and was told of the plot against the Jews. Mordecai also told Esther that she needed to approach the king and "plead before him for her people" (Esther 4:8). This was the big test for Esther. It was well known that if anyone appeared before the king unbidden, they would be put to death. The only exception was if the king held out his golden scepter. But no one knew if the king would.

To pile on the pressure, Mordecai told Esther that God is faithful and would deliver His people, even if she chose not to go to the king. But he also told her that she and her "father's house will perish" (Esther 4:14). Then he added perhaps the most well-known question from the Book of Esther in verse 14: "Yet who knows whether you have come to the kingdom for such a time as this?"

It was then left for Esther to choose. She could have chosen to remain safely where she was, never revealing her lineage or the plot against her people, but it would have only been a temporary safety. Instead, Esther chose to remain loyal— to God, to Mordecai who raised her, and to her people, regardless of what happened to her. I love how she asked all of her people to fast and pray for her and then drew her line in the sand in verse 16: "and if I perish, I perish!"

So, Esther and her maidservants (and her people) fasted and prayed. On the third day, Esther put on her royal robes (she took heart!) and stood in the face of death to do what was right. And God gave Esther favor with the king. The king saw her and held out his golden scepter. Esther remained loyal, even unto death. She was granted life and saved her people.

We have such a wonderful example in Esther of maintaining a loyal heart to our King.

We also have some interesting things in common with Esther. We have been chosen by our King. He has called us for such a time as this to follow Him. Esther's behavior throughout her life—her loyal heart to God—was what made her truly beautiful.

But here is where we are NOT like Esther. She had to appear before her king, not knowing how he would respond to her. We, on the other hand, know how our King will respond! In fact, our King calls us to come to Him! He continually holds out the scepter to us, beckoning us to come to Him—with our cares, our troubles, our burdens, and everything else, so He can welcome us and give us rest. He always grants us an audience. Let us remain loyal, take heart in every circumstance, go to Jesus our King, and stand in His presence. He will receive us!

Dear God, thank You for the beautiful example I have in Esther to be loyal in heart and to take heart, no matter what I face. Thank You that I can know that because of Jesus, You will always hear my prayers and receive me. In Jesus' Name, Amen.

Areas Where I Need to Take Heart:

_____

_____

_____

_____

_____

_____

_____

Chapter 4

Discipline: The Proverbs 31 Woman

❦

"Give her the fruit of her hands." Proverbs 31:31

The virtuous wife in Proverbs 31 has long been a standard of excellence for women everywhere. As we read each verse, we discover more and more about the character of this woman and how she conducts herself on a daily basis. But before we look more closely at the virtuous wife, let's briefly look at a woman mentioned at the start of Chapter 31 in Proverbs, the king's mother.

The first nine verses in Proverbs 31 are advice to a king from his mother. She is instructing her son on the ways a king should be disciplined—because he must be able to think clearly to judge rightly and stand up for the weak and needy. Discipline was clearly recognized by the king's mother as essential to a king justly ruling.

In our culture, discipline tends to be a negative word. We often associate it with punishment for wrongdoing, and that is part of its definition. However, discipline also means a training of conduct and implies the development of self-control. The word disciple comes from the Old English word, discipul, * which describes someone who learns from another by following them. This word was specifically meant to describe followers of Jesus. Discipline and disciple go hand-in-hand with the idea of self-control. In fact, in Luke 9:23, Jesus says, "If anyone desires to come after Me, let him deny himself, and take up his cross daily, and follow Me."

The virtuous wife we read about in Proverbs 31 is a woman of discipline. She rises early and takes care of her household (verse 15). This brings to mind Psalm 5:3: "My voice You shall hear in the morning, O Lord; In the morning I will direct it to You, and I will look up." As spiritual warrior women, one of the most important ways to take care of our households is to begin our days with prayer—first thing—before we dive into the day and the countless tasks ahead of us!

The Proverbs 31 woman uses her time wisely "and her lamp does not go out by night" (verse 18). Time is one of those precious commodities that is so easily wasted, and, once gone, cannot be recovered. Sometimes this is a hard truth to face, but we must. Especially in our modern world of constant distractions, we need to remain disciplined and vigilant to guard ourselves and our families against the pitfalls of the digital age. We need wisdom and discernment.

In verse 16, we read how the virtuous wife "considers a field and buys it; from her profits she plants a vineyard." Here also is wisdom and discernment. This woman obviously knows a good business opportunity when she sees it. She is able to look ahead and gauge potential. But we also know she does nothing out of vanity or for selfish gain; she is on a mission to care for those in her domain—her family, her maidservants, and those in need around her. "She watches over the ways of her household, and does not eat the bread of idleness" (verse 27). She is willing to pray hard and work hard for her family and her husband knows he can count on her: "The heart of her husband safely trusts her; she will have no lack of gain" (verse 11). God blesses this woman because of her faithfulness.

I also want to point out the Proverbs 31 woman did not neglect taking care of herself: "She girds herself with strength, and strengthens her arms" (verse 17). This implies that she kept herself healthy, both spiritually and physically, not because she was egocentric, but because she wanted to be adequately prepared to fulfill her mission. As spiritual warrior women, Jesus must take first priority in our individual lives. If we put Him first, in every aspect, then we will be able to love our husbands, our children, our families, and others in the right way.

As you read through Proverbs 31, notice how the virtuous woman's appearance is not really described, except that "her clothing is fine linen and purple" (verse 22). Fine linen is often used to symbolize righteousness. "And to her it was granted to be arrayed in fine linen, clean and bright, for the fine linen is the righteous acts of the saints" (Revelation 19:8). Purple is a color typically associated with wealth and royalty. So, the description of the virtuous woman's appearance is not her physical beauty, per se, it is her spiritual condition. "Strength and honor are her clothing..." (verse 25). She is a righteous woman and is of noble character—a representation of a daughter of the King. Even in the way she speaks: "She opens her mouth with wisdom. And on her tongue is the law of kindness" (verse 26). So, everything about this woman, inside and out, honors the Lord.

We have so many lessons we can learn from Proverbs 31 and all the virtuous wife exemplifies. It is clear that her behaviors, decisions, and the motivations behind them are a regular part of her daily life–not one-time actions. She has become disciplined in living a life that pleases the Lord. The last verse of Proverbs describes her reward: "Give her the fruit of her hands." Let us, as spiritual warrior women, pray for God to do such a work in us.

Dear God, help me to be like the woman in Proverbs 31. It seems like such a high standard to meet and I know that on my own it is impossible, but with You it is possible. Please work in me so that I am clothed in white linen with Your righteousness. Help me to honor You in all I do, in the words I speak, and in the decisions I make. In Jesus' Name, Amen.

Ways that God is Shaping Me into a Proverbs 31 Woman:

_____

_____

_____

_____

_____

_____

_____

_____

_____

*Referenced from etymonline.com

Chapter 5

Patience: Anna

"And coming up at that very hour she began to give thanks to God and to speak of Him to all who were waiting for the redemption of Jerusalem." Luke 2:38, ESV

Anna was a prophetess. After only seven years of marriage, her husband died, leaving her a widow. She "did not depart from the temple, worshiping with fasting and prayer night and day" (Luke 2:37, ESV). We don't know exactly how many years Anna spent in the temple, but since she was young when her husband died, and 84 years old at the time described by Luke, it was most likely 60 years or more.

For us modern-day women, living like Anna is probably a little hard to imagine. To spend several decades of days and nights, praying, fasting, and worshiping is quite remarkable. Our days and nights tend to be hectic and non-stop from the moment we get out of bed until we pass out on our pillows. But we can glean some important insights on living the life of a spiritual warrior woman from Anna because she was one.

Anna was content with where God had her. She was not out to please anyone other than God. She spent her life in worship. Isn't this how we should also live—wherever God has us? If we take time to consider who God is and all He has done, we should respond with absolute praise! Psalm 29:2 says, "Give unto the Lord the glory due His name; Worship the Lord in the beauty of holiness" (NKJV). When we start to recognize the goodness of God, it leads us to repentance (Romans 2:4). Repentance is a turning of the heart away from sin and toward God. It includes a right change in thinking and behavior. To truly become spiritual warrior women like Anna, we want to live in a state of worship, seeing God's goodness, and continually turning to Him in how we think and live.

Now let's look at something else Anna did regularly—she fasted. Fasting is too often overlooked in our modern western church society, or perhaps is not taken seriously enough. However, as you read throughout both Old and New Testaments, you see that it is an important and regular part of a fruitful prayer life. We find that it is done to draw closer to God, to cry out to Him for help, to be humble before Him, and to mourn. Fasting is something we are supposed to do. The Bible does not say, "if" you fast, it says "when." Matthew 6:17-18 tells us: "But you, when you fast, anoint your head and wash your face, so that you do not appear to men to be fasting, but to your Father who is in the secret place; and your Father who sees in secret will reward you openly." We don't need to make a big production or social media announcement about it, but leave it between God and us. Sincere, heartfelt fasting is worthwhile.

Finally, Anna was continually in prayer. We can do this as well. As we drive, shower, work, cook, clean, walk, or whatever we are doing, we can have our hearts calling out to our Father.

1 Thessalonians 5:17 tells us we are to "pray without ceasing." This should be, like Anna, how we live. Prayer is our lifeline to God. Look at the beginning of Luke 18: "Then [Jesus] spoke a parable to them, that men always ought to pray and not lose heart." And you know what the parable was? It was the parable of the persistent widow! Like Anna, the widow in the parable is so persistent (and patient I might add) that even a judge who did not fear God grants her request. How much more is our Heavenly Father going to listen to our prayers? Persistence and patience are important because we are trusting God to hear our prayers. We can rest in confidence knowing He hears us when we cry out to Him. Hebrews 4:16 reminds us: "Let us therefore come boldly to the throne of grace, that we may obtain mercy and grace to help in time of need."

A life of prayer brings with it hope and confidence in God that He does, indeed, keep His promises. Anna's life of patient dedication to God resulted in her seeing, face to face, just how true this is. We read this in Luke 2:38. Some versions say that Anna came up at the very *instant* that Simeon was speaking to Mary about Jesus. Anna got to see our Savior with her very own eyes and then proclaim Him to those around her. This was no chance meeting. It was the ultimate divine appointment—the beautiful reward of Anna's patient lifelong dedication.

We too, are waiting to see our Savior with our very own eyes, and one day we will! Let us take a lesson from Anna, and live out our days for Jesus in worship, fasting, and prayer. Then we too, will receive that beautiful reward.

Dear God, help me to live a life of worship, fasting, and prayer, patiently waiting on You. Turn my heart always toward You. I am looking forward to the day when I see You with my own eyes. In Jesus' Name, Amen.

What I Praise God for:

_____

_____

_____

_____

_____

_____

_____

_____

_____

Chapter 6

Faith: The Woman Who Touched Jesus' Hem

"Daughter, your faith has made you well. Go in peace and be healed of your affliction." Mark 5:34

You've heard her story. Twelve long years with an issue of blood. No relief. No hope. Could you imagine how she felt? Despairing, exhausted, anemic, miserable. Probably embarrassed too. She was considered "unclean" according to Leviticus 15:25, so she had to live with that on top of everything else. This woman did not have any of the modern conveniences we have today, which would also have limited where she was able to go and what she was able to do. We read about her in the Books of Matthew, Mark, and Luke. In Matthew, it describes her condition as diseased (9:20 KJV). Mark 5:26 tells us she "had

35

suffered many things from many physicians" and was, in fact, getting worse. Luke further explains that she had spent all of her living—her life savings—for nothing.

I wonder what effort and struggle it took for this woman to brave the crowds and work her way through the mob of people to get close to Jesus. Maybe she realized she would be unable to get close enough to speak to Him. She knew who He was; she recognized His authority and power. She was desperate for whatever she could get. In Matthew 9:20-21 we read: "...[she] came behind Him, and touched the hem of His garment. For she said within herself, If I may but touch His garment, I shall be whole" (ESV). For her, it was enough to just reach out and touch the very edge of Jesus' garment. What an act of humility that demonstrated her faith! She knew Jesus was the source of healing and life and yet, she felt that simply touching the hem of His garment would be enough.

As we read in Mark's account, as soon as she touched Jesus' garment, "the flow of blood dried up, and she felt in her body that she was healed of her disease." Wow! What must that have been like? All of the suffering and humiliation gone in an instant. But then, we read how Jesus, "perceiving in Himself that power had gone from Him, immediately turned about in the crowd and said, 'Who touched my garments?'" Notice how specific this is. Jesus knew. There were probably lots of people surrounding Him and touching Him while this took place. Even His disciples wondered why Jesus wanted to know who touched Him. But in this account, that isn't what Jesus asked. He said,

"Who touched my garments?" He knew that someone had put their faith in Him and had been healed.

Imagine what the woman must have felt when Jesus asked this! Maybe she thought He wouldn't notice, or maybe she just didn't even consider this possibility. Look how she comes to Jesus in Mark 5:33: "But the woman, knowing what had happened to her, came in fear and trembling and fell down before Him and told Him the whole truth." Perhaps she thought she was in trouble, but she laid it all on the line anyway—just put it out there and threw herself on His mercy in front of everyone. She was desperate enough that she didn't care what anyone was going to think that's for sure! Since she already recognized Jesus' authority that He could heal her, it must have struck her immensely more when she heard Him say that He knew someone (she) had touched His garments. She told Him everything and waited for His response. Jesus said to her, "Daughter, your faith has made you well; go in peace, and be healed of your disease."

He called her daughter! He accepted her as His own. Then He told her that her faith had made her well— like giving an answer of yes to a prayer. Then with that, came a blessing: "go in peace, and be healed of your disease." Jesus did not want her to worry anymore. He wasn't angry with her for sneaking in there and touching His hem. He knew it was a true act of faith for her and He responded with a blessing.

Jesus is looking for true acts of faith from us. First and

foremost, we must answer the question: Have you trusted JesusChrist to be your Lord and Savior and forgive your sins? This step is necessary to be a Christian and receive eternal life. Jesus says in John 14:6, "I am the way, the truth, and the life. No one comes to the Father except through Me." And we certainly cannot be good enough to enter Heaven. We know this is true if we are honest with ourselves. But also look at what verses 8 and 9 tell us in 1 John: "If we say we have no sin, we deceive ourselves, and the truth is not in us. If we confess our sins, He is faithful and just to forgive us our sins and to cleanse us from all unrighteousness." We need that cleansing and forgiveness for our spiritual healing, which is of infinitely more importance than our physical healing here in this life. However, we can and should pray for physical healing too, while knowing that sometimes God uses a long-term illness or suffering of some sort to bring us to a desperation that makes us cry out like we never would otherwise. Just like the woman in the Bible, so desperate, yet full of faith, willing to just touch the hem of the Savior's garment and know it is enough.

It is interesting to note that ancient tradition placed significance on the hem of a garment. This offers us a wonderful parallel. The significance of the hem in this story is that a hem without Jesus is nothing. Just like religion without Jesus is nothing. It is always about Jesus. We need Him. We need the healing and cleansing of our Savior. All we have to do is sincerely and humbly reach out to our Lord, and He will receive us, bless us, and give us peace in return, just as He did for the woman who touched His hem.

We must ask ourselves if we are both full of faith and desperate for Jesus. Perhaps you are in the midst of a long, relentless illness, or a difficult situation with no end in sight. Will you allow the pain of these circumstances drive you to fall on your knees before the Lord in absolute humility and desperation, confess all, and receive His blessing?

Dear God, You know my need and You know my situation. I cry out to You for healing and deliverance. Please help me have true faith in You. Please give me peace. In Jesus' Name, Amen.

My Needs and What the Bible Says About Them:

_____

_____

_____

_____

_____

_____

_____

_____

_____

_____

Chapter 7

Surrender: Mary

"Behold the maidservant of the Lord! Let it be to me according to your word." Luke 1:38

In the book of Luke, we read how Mary, who was already expecting Jesus, traveled to visit her relative, Elizabeth. Elizabeth was also expecting a child, who would later be known as John the Baptist. Upon Mary's arrival, we read, "And it happened, when Elizabeth heard the greeting of Mary, that the babe leaped in her womb; and Elizabeth was filled with the Holy Spirit." Then Elizabeth prophesied over Mary, saying "Blessed are you among women, and blessed is the fruit of your womb!" Elizabeth also told Mary, "Blessed is she who believed, for there will be a fulfillment of those things which were told her from the Lord." Mary responded with her now famous words found in the first chapter of the book of Luke. These words, known as the

Song of Mary, begin with the verse: "My soul magnifies the Lord, and my spirit has rejoiced in God my Savior." They go on to describe how wonderful and mighty God is and they tell of incredible things He has done for Israel, all generations, and for Mary herself.

No doubt Mary knew she was incredibly blessed by God. What an honor and a tremendous responsibility. Which begs the questions: Who was this young woman? What was it about her that she found such favor with God? We see a glimpse of what kind of person she was when we read how she responded to the Archangel Gabriel's news of what was about to happen to her.

After Gabriel explained what was going to take place, Mary's response was simple yet profound. Mary said in Luke 1:38, "Behold the maidservant of the Lord! Let it be to me according to your word." In this one statement, we see in Mary an attribute that we all need—especially if we want to grow deeper in our prayer lives and walks with Jesus. This attribute is surrender. First, she responded to Gabriel, "Behold the maidservant of the Lord!" Here, Mary was not only recognizing God's authority over her and her life, but she also acknowledged that she was His willing servant. Then Mary declared, "Let it be to me according to your word." In this declaration, Mary surrendered her life and her own will to that of the Father's. She was willing to accept whatever God had in mind for her. She didn't add anything from her own personal wish list or put restrictions or conditions on her acceptance. She surrendered her whole life to Him.

We need to adopt this principle of surrender in our own lives. How many times do we pray with our own agendas in mind? Are we willing to accept—without condition—what God has for us?

Mary certainly didn't foresee then all of the heartache that would come with Jesus' death on the cross. But she also couldn't know the joy that would follow His absolute victory over sin and death. The thing is, she didn't need to. She simply surrendered all. She was willing to give her life completely to the Lord's will and trust completely in His goodness and mercy. Mary mentioned this when she visited Elizabeth. In Luke 1:50, she said, "And His mercy is on those who fear Him from generation to generation." Mary feared the Lord. She was in awe of Him.

The Bible is full of amazing promises for those who fear the Lord. Proverbs 19:23 says, "The fear of the Lord leads to life, and he who has it will abide in satisfaction. He will not be visited with evil." In Proverbs 14:26 we read: "In the fear of the Lord there is strong confidence, and His children will have a place of refuge." Look at this one in Psalms 25:14: "The friendship of the Lord is for those who fear Him, and He makes known to them His covenant." Mary would have been familiar with these promises. Because she feared the Lord, she knew she could trust Him completely with her life. And He even made known His covenant to her! Look again at what Gabriel told Mary in Luke Chapter 1: "And behold, you will conceive in your womb and bear a son, and you shall call His name Jesus. He will be great and will

43

be called the Son of the Most High. And the Lord God will give to Him the throne of His father David, and He will reign over the house of Jacob forever, and of His Kingdom there will be no end."

Let's follow Mary's example and be in awe of our magnificent Heavenly Father. Let us trust Him completely and put our entire lives in His hands. We can count on His mercy that is promised in Luke 1:50 to "those who fear Him from generation to generation." May our responses to God be with the same surrender as Mary: "Behold the maidservant of the Lord! Let it be to me according to your word."

Dear God, I place myself wholly in Your hands. Let Your will be done in my life. In Jesus' Name, Amen.

I Am in Awe of God About:

_____

_____

_____

_____

_____

_____

_____

_____

_____

Chapter 8

Obedience: Ruth

"Your people shall be my people, And your God, my God."
Ruth 1:16

Ruth was a young woman from the land of Moab. She was not born as one of the children of Israel. Even though she married into one of the families, she was still not truly one of them—yet. The children of Israel did not typically marry outsiders. But after the death of Elimelech, who had brought his family to Moab from Judah due to famine, each of his two sons took a wife from the young women of Moab. Ruth was one of them.

I imagine Ruth heard all about the God of Israel from her husband and her mother-in-law, Naomi. Surely, the wonderful stories of God delivering His people were continual topics of conversation around the dinner table and during household tasks throughout the ten years they lived together in Moab. The stories must have been awe-inspiring to a young woman from one of Israel's neighboring lands.

Ruth's husband and his brother both died, leaving Ruth, her mother-in-law, and her sister-in-law on their own. In grief and bitterness of heart, Naomi, Ruth's mother-in-law, decided to return to Bethlehem in the land of Judah. I think Naomi must have been close to both of her daughters-in-law, because as she bid them goodbye, the Bible tells us, "they lifted up their voices and wept." (Twice, in fact.) Both daughters-in-law professed their desire to follow Naomi to Judah, but only one was truly serious—Ruth.

She eloquently declared in Ruth 1:16-17: "Entreat me not to leave you, or to turn back from following after you; For wherever you go, I will go; And wherever you lodge, I will lodge; Your people shall be my people, And your God, my God. Where you die, I will die, and there I will be buried. The Lord do so to me, and more also, if anything but death parts you and me." This beautiful speech displayed Ruth's heart, not only toward her mother-in-law, but toward the God of Israel. Ruth made a choice of obedience. She would have clearly known what it meant to become part of Naomi's people and to make God her God. Ruth willingly chose a life of obedience to the Lord.

As we read more of Ruth's story, we see her obedience was not short lived, but was a lifelong hallmark of her character. She sought after and followed Naomi's wisdom.

46

First, she asked Naomi's permission to glean in the fields of Boaz, a wealthy relative of Elimelech's. The fact that Ruth went to glean in the fields during harvest tells us she and Naomi were poor. After all, they were both widows and had returned to Naomi's homeland after a lengthy absence. So, Ruth followed behind the harvesters and gathered the heads of grain leftover and fallen to the wayside. As she worked, Ruth must have caught Boaz's eye, because he inquired after her. He later spoke to her and told her to glean only in his fields, where she would be protected and provided with water.

When Ruth asked why he would do this for her, Boaz explained that he had heard of her faithfulness to Naomi and to the God of Israel: "It has been fully reported to me, all that you have done for your mother-in-law since the death of your husband, and how you have left your father and mother and the land of your birth, and have come to a people whom you did not know before. The Lord repay your work, and a full reward be given you by the Lord God of Israel, under whose wings you have sought refuge." Wow! What an acknowledgement and blessing. But Boaz went even further. He instructed his young men to allow her to glean without reproach and to do so from among the sheaves (more favor for Ruth). Boaz also ordered them to let extra grain fall on purpose so Ruth could have it.

When Naomi heard of Boaz's favor toward Ruth, she gave specific instructions that Ruth faithfully carried out.

As a result, Ruth became the wife of Boaz. The Bible describes all that took place. It was known as a custom of redemption. Boaz purchased all that had belonged to Elimelech and kept the name and lineage from being cut off. Boaz restored all that had been lost upon Elimelech's death. Boaz rescued and redeemed it all—including Ruth!

Ruth's story is our story. We are all lost and in need of redemption. We need someone to pay the price for us and make us His own. And we have Someone. His name is Jesus. He paid the price for us. When we choose to follow Him—when we choose a life of obedience like Ruth—He rescues, redeems, and saves us! But it is a decision we must make, the way Ruth had to decide to go with Naomi in the first place. Ruth chose to follow God and live a life of obedience to Him. And God accepted Ruth and placed her into the lineage that led to Obed, Jesse, David, and ultimately, Jesus.

Ruth made a life-changing decision when she chose to go with Naomi. It was a fork in the road with eternal consequences. Ruth had no idea of the immeasurable blessings that awaited her. She was free to choose either way, but only one way led to the Savior. Ruth's obedience then and after gave her a beautiful inheritance.

If we want to be true spiritual warrior women, we have a decision to make. It's the same fork-in-the-road choice Ruth faced. Like her, we are free to choose either way. But only one way leads to salvation. We must choose to take refuge in Jesus Christ and faithfully follow Him in obedience.

When we do, He redeems us, makes us His own, and give us, too, a beautiful inheritance.

Dear God, I choose You. I choose a life of following You in obedience. Help me be Your obedient daughter. Lead and guide me and let me always take refuge in You. Thank You for redeeming me. In Jesus' Name, Amen.

Areas of My Life Where I Want to be More Obedient to the Lord:

_____

_____

_____

_____

_____

_____

_____

_____

_____

Chapter 9

Wisdom: Priscilla

❧

"When Aquila and Priscilla heard him, they took him aside and explained to him the way of God more accurately." Acts 18:26

Priscilla is a woman of wisdom mentioned in the New Testament. We first hear of her in the Book of Acts. Paul had come to Corinth from Athens, Greece and found Aquila, a Jewish man exiled from Rome with his wife, who was Priscilla. In verses two and three, we learn that he came to Aquila and Priscilla, and "because [Paul] was of the same trade, he stayed with them and worked; for by occupation they were tentmakers."

When someone stays with you in your house and works alongside you, there is ample time to become well acquainted and have plenty of discussions. We can assume Paul, Aquila, and Priscilla discussed all that had happened in Paul's life and Aquila and Priscilla's too. Imagine what it would have been like to talk about all their shared history as fellow Jews, and all they knew of the scriptures and the Messiah. Priscilla must have learned so much from the time Paul spent with her and her husband. We can also assume Priscilla and Aquila became his good friends. We have an idea of this because we read in Acts 18:18-19 that Paul took them with him when he sailed to Syria. He left Aquila and Priscilla in Ephesus and promised to return to them if God willed it.

Aquila and Priscilla were likely the ones others looked to among the Christians in Ephesus. The wisdom and spiritual understanding they gained from being around Jesus' Apostle surely equipped them to help others grow in the Lord. In fact, Acts 18:24-26 tells us about a man named Apollos who "spoke and taught accurately the things of the Lord, though he knew only of the baptism of John." Then, we read how after Apollos boldly spoke in the synagogue, Aquila and Priscilla "took him aside and explained to him the way of God more accurately."

What a great example of a spiritual warrior woman of wisdom we are given in Priscilla. First, we know she was more than just a bystander. Priscilla was an industrious worker alongside her husband in their family business of tent-making. She was a follower of Jesus who was granted special time to learn directly from the Apostle Paul. The fact that Paul took Priscilla and her husband Aquila with him to Ephesus shows that he knew the depth of both of their relationships with Jesus. In Romans 16:3, Paul calls Priscilla and Aquila his "fellow workers in Christ Jesus." He knew they would be wise leaders for the church in Ephesus, which may be why the Bible says he left them there when he departed for Jerusalem. We have evidence of their leadership in 1 Corinthians 16:19 when Paul writes, "Aquila and Priscilla greet you heartily in the Lord, with the church that is in their house." So, here we have Priscilla, a former businesswoman, trained for ministry by Paul the Apostle, serving the Lord with her husband in a church in their home.

What makes Priscilla so interesting is that we don't know details of things she may have said or done, but what we do know about her shows us she was a faithful servant of Jesus, full of wisdom, and she honored Him with it. We see this in how she and her husband helped to teach Apollos. They were wiser in the things of the Lord. They both had the wisdom to discern that he spoke the truth accurately and sincerely, but just didn't have the whole story. So, Aquila and Priscilla, together, taught Apollos what he needed to know so he could continue boldly sharing the whole Gospel correctly. We know God sent Paul to her and her husband for a time and then placed her as a leader, along with Aquila, in one of the earliest churches in Asia, and they hosted it in their home!

Wisdom is a gift from God, that He freely gives. James 1:5 says, "If any of you lacks wisdom, let him ask God, who gives generously to all without reproach, and it will be given him" (ESV). Let us, as spiritual warrior women, ask God to give us wisdom. It is foundational for an effective prayer life. Proverbs 24:3 tells us, "By wisdom a house is built, and by understanding it is established..." We need wisdom to be prepared for how God wants to use us. We need wisdom to know what and how to pray. And we need wisdom so we may know "what is the hope of His calling, what are the riches of the glory of His inheritance in the saints, and what is the exceeding greatness of His power toward us who believe, according to the working of His mighty power..." (Ephesians 1:18-19, NKJV). Let us pray for wisdom, so we can obtain spiritual discernment and understanding, and like Priscilla, so we can serve the Lord wherever we are and wherever He sends us. We want to be ready to help others, teaching them to understand the "way of God more accurately."

Dear God, I ask You to give me wisdom, so I may know You better. Please give me spiritual understanding so I may know and do Your will, and teach others to do the same. In Jesus' Name, Amen.

What Else the Bible Has to Say About the Importance of Wisdom:

_____

_____

_____

_____

_____

_____

Chapter 10

Discernment: Rahab

"...for the Lord your God, He is God in heaven above and on earth beneath." Joshua 2:11

Before the famous battle of Jericho, Joshua sent two spies to scope out the land. Scripture tells us, "they went, and came to the house of a harlot named Rahab, and lodged there." The next thing we read is that the king of Jericho sent word to Rahab and told her to hand over the spies. But Rahab did not. She hid the spies and then misled the king's men so they would not catch them. At this point, we might be wondering why Rahab would first, provide lodging to men she must have known were enemies of her people who were about to invade? And second, why would she disobey her king's order and lie to protect the spies? What was going on with Rahab that made her so bold in her actions? Surely, she was risking her life, her family, and her possessions. She must have known something, or she would not have acted as she did.

We find the answers in Joshua 2, beginning in verse 9. When Rahab hid the spies underneath the stalks of flax on her roof and said, "I know that the Lord has given you the land, that the terror of you has fallen on us, and that all the inhabitants of the land are fainthearted because of you." She then told them how she heard about the parting of the Red Sea and their defeat of the Amorites. Rahab then made a statement that shows she discerned the truth. In verse 11 she declared, "for the Lord your God, He is God in heaven above and on earth beneath." She recognized God and His power. She understood that there was no stopping the will of God. Rahab believed in the God of Israel and recognized that she needed to be on His side.

Rahab's discernment also made her bold. She asked the spies to make an oath before the Lord that she and her family be spared when they conquered the land. The spies swore they would as long as she tied a cord of scarlet in her window and all who were to be saved remained within her house. They promised to deal kindly with her and her family. There is a definite picture here for us of being saved from destruction by the blood of Jesus. As long as Rahab and her family remained under the protection of the scarlet cord, they would be saved. They did and they were. In fact, in Joshua 6:17, Joshua himself says, "Now the city shall be doomed by the Lord to destruction, it and all who are in it. Only the harlot shall live, she all who are with her in the house, because she hid the messengers that we sent." So, Rahab and her family were saved.

Rahab herself received great blessings too. We have our first hint in Joshua 6:25: "And Joshua spared Rahab the harlot, her father's household, and all that she had. So, she dwells in Israel to this day, because she hid the messengers whom Joshua sent to spy out Jericho." So, Rahab the harlot was taken in by the children of Israel. And there's more. Rahab is honored in the New Testament. In Hebrews 11:31, Paul writes, "By faith the harlot Rahab did not perish with those who did not believe, when she had received the spies with peace." James 2:25 uses Rahab as an example for living: "Likewise was not Rahab the harlot also justified by works when she received the messengers and sent them out another way?" And finally, she is named in the lineage of Jesus in Matthew 1:5: "Salmon begat Boaz by Rahab, Obed begot Jesse, and Jesse begot David the King." Incredible!

Because Rahab discerned the truth about who God is, she had faith in Him and acted on it. By God's grace she and her family were saved, and she was grafted into the bloodline of the Savior! What a wonderful example of the importance of discernment. We need the weapon of discernment to be effective spiritual warrior women. Romans 12:2 tells us, "Do not be conformed to this world, but be transformed by the renewal of your mind, that by testing you may discern what is the will of God, what is good and acceptable and perfect."

With discernment, we will know better how to pray and what to pray. We can learn how to recognize what the will of God is and then act on it. Discernment is a powerful weapon. It is needed for us to be able to understand the things of the Lord that are spiritually discerned according to 1 Corinthians 2:14 and needed for us to be able to judge rightly according to John 7:24. For Rahab, discernment led to her acting on faith, which led to her and her family being saved from destruction in one of the greatest battles in history. For us, we are amidst a spiritual battle, fighting for ourselves and those we love. We need to obtain and wield the God-given gift of discernment to be true spiritual warrior women who know, like Rahab knew, that: "He is God in heaven above and on earth beneath."

Dear God, I pray for the gift of discernment. Help me to recognize what is Your will. Please help me to be guided by the Holy Spirit in every area of my life and know that You are God in heaven above and on earth beneath. In Jesus' Name, Amen.

What Else the Bible Has to Say About Discernment:

_____

_____

_____

_____

_____

_____

Chapter 11

Forgiveness: The Woman About to be Stoned

"Neither do I condemn you; go and sin no more." John 8:11

The account of the woman about to be stoned is a significant point in Jesus' ministry. In John 8, we read of how she was brought to Jesus and placed before Him, apparently in front of a large crowd, since Jesus was teaching in the temple at that moment. The scribes and Pharisees wanted to trap Jesus and find something they could use against Him. They said they caught the woman in adultery and then proceeded to quote Moses at Jesus.

His response was incredible.

First, He ignored them and simply stooped down and drew on the ground. When they persisted in asking, Jesus rose up and made an amazing statement: "He who is without sin among you, let him throw a stone at her first." Next, in verse 8, we read how Jesus stooped down and started drawing on the ground again! Verse 9 tells us, "Then those who heard it, being convicted by their own conscience, went out one by one, beginning with the oldest even to the last." When only Jesus and the adulterous woman remained, Jesus said to her: "Woman, where are those accusers of yours? Has no one condemned you?" She responded that there was no one, and referred to Jesus as Lord. Jesus' next words in verse 11 are even more astounding than before, especially understanding that the Jews at that time strictly followed Mosaic law (which demanded death by stoning for adultery): "And Jesus said to her, 'Neither do I condemn you; go and sin no more.'" Wow. Jesus did not condemn her, although He had every right to. He granted her forgiveness and released her from a death sentence. And then He told her to "go and sin no more." By saying this, He was telling this woman that she was forgiven, and it was time to follow Him. Look what Jesus said afterward to the people still in the temple in verse 12: "Then Jesus spoke to them again, saying, 'I am the light of the world. He who follows Me shall not walk in darkness, but have the light of life."

The adulterous woman surely felt as if she stepped from darkness into light after Jesus saved her from death, forgave her, and told her to follow Him by not living a life of sin anymore. This raises some important points that come with forgiveness. First, there must be an acknowledgement of wrongdoing. 1 John

1:9 tells us, "If we confess our sins, He is faithful and just to forgive our sins..." We must confess to the Lord. This implies repentance, meaning we sincerely desire to turn away from sin and turn to God. He knows our hearts. He knows when we truly mean something. And when we do, He is ready and waiting to freely forgive us. And being the wonderful God He is, He doesn't stop there. The rest of 1 John 1:9 says He will "...cleanse us from all unrighteousness." Beautiful! He doesn't leave us there. He bids us to follow Him and walk in His light.

As we follow Jesus, He makes us like Him. 2 Corinthians 5:17 gives us this promise: "Therefore, if anyone is in Christ, he is a new creation; old things have passed away; behold, all things have become new." I love this because when Jesus forgives, He does so completely. He doesn't tell us to "go and now constantly dwell on how awful you have been and feel guilty." No, He says "go and sin no more." In other words, don't look back—but also, don't go back. Jesus sets us free to follow Him through forgiveness. And it is not because we deserve it—we don't! Like the woman caught in adultery, we are guilty. We know this. Which makes God's forgiveness toward us through Jesus that much more astonishing. Micah 7:18-19 describes God's forgiveness this way: "Who is a God like you, pardoning iniquity and passing over transgression for the remnant of His inheritance? He does not retain His anger forever, because He delights in steadfast love. He will again have compassion on us; He will tread our iniquities underfoot. [He] will cast all our sins into the depths of the sea" (ESV).

And since Jesus has forgiven us so wonderfully, we are not supposed to let it stop with ourselves. He wants us to extend the same type of forgiveness to others, too. In the Lord's prayer it says, "and forgive us our debts, as we also have forgiven our debtors" (Matthew 6:12). In verses 14 and 15 Jesus also says, "For if you forgive others their trespasses, your Heavenly Father will also forgive you, but if you do not forgive others their trespasses, neither will your Father forgive your trespasses." Ok, now let that sink in. We will be forgiven the way we forgive. Since Jesus has paid for all our sins and then freely forgiven us for ours, how could we do any less? Especially if we desire a fruitful and effective prayer life, then we MUST forgive—we have no other option. In Mark 11:25 Jesus says, "And whenever you stand praying, forgive, if you have anything against anyone, so that your Father also who is in heaven may forgive you your trespasses."

To be true spiritual warrior women, we need to be forgiven ourselves, and then extend that same forgiveness to others. Jesus freely offers forgiveness of sin though He has every right to condemn us. But because of His great love and His sacrifice, He sets us free to follow Him and to "go and sin no more."

Dear God, please forgive me of my sins and help me to freely forgive others. Help me to follow after You more every day and walk in the light as You are in the light. In Jesus' Name, Amen.

Forgiveness I Need to Extend:

_____

_____

_____

_____

_____

_____

_____

_____

_____

_____

Chapter 12

Sacrifice: Hannah

"...the Lord has granted me my petition of which I asked of Him." 1 Samuel 1:27

Imagine praying for something you desired for many, many years. You ached, you cried, you prayed some more. Finally, your prayer was answered, and you received what you had long awaited. Joy! Now, imagine not keeping your beautiful gift, but willingly and gladly giving it back to the one who gave it to you. This is what Hannah did.

We are introduced to Hannah in 1 Samuel 1. She was one of the two wives of Elkanah and unable to bear children—a point of contention for Hannah. Not only did she long to be a mother, but the other wife (whom the Bible calls her rival) provoked her year after year. By the time we meet Hannah, she is beyond comfort. Even her husband's favor toward her is no balm for her wounded soul. We read how she went to the tabernacle of the Lord. In verse 10 it says, "And she was in bitterness of soul, and prayed to the Lord and wept in anguish." After that, in verse 11, Hannah vowed to the Lord that if He gave her a son, she would give him to the Lord "all the days of his life, and no razor shall come upon his head." So, Hannah promised that if God gave her a son, she would dedicate that son to God, and he would serve God in a special way all his life.

While Hannah was pouring out her heart to the Lord, Eli, the high priest, came to her and accused her of being drunk! But she gently responded, "Do not consider your maidservant a wicked woman, for out of the abundance of my complaint and grief I have spoken until now." In verse 17 we read, "Then Eli answered and said, 'Go in peace, and the God of Israel grant your petition which you have asked of Him.'"

And God did. Not long after, Hannah gave birth to a son. Imagine her relief, joy, gratitude, and feelings of exoneration! She could have triumphed over her rival and let it go to her head, but she did not. She could have forgotten her promise to God in all her excitement, but Hannah did not. We see this in verse 20: "...Hannah conceived and bore a son, and called his name Samuel, saying, 'Because I have asked for him from the Lord.'"

When Samuel was old enough to be weaned, Hannah took him to the temple to Eli. When she met the high priest again, she told him, "I am the woman who stood by you here, praying to the Lord. For this child I prayed, and the Lord has granted me my petition which I asked of Him. Therefore, I also have lent him to the Lord; as long as he lives he shall be lent to the Lord" (26-28). They then worshiped the Lord. Hannah's beautiful prayer is written in the next chapter. So, Hannah and her husband gave Samuel to the Lord and returned home. In Chapter 2 verse 11 we read, "...the child ministered to the Lord before Eli the priest."

Oh, what Hannah must have felt! I imagine she felt joy but also missed her little son. She loved him dearly, of course, and was no doubt grateful for the time she spent with him. We know Hannah never stopped loving Samuel or remembering him. According to verse 19, she "used to make him a little robe and bring it to him year by year when she came up with her husband to offer the yearly sacrifice."

So, Hannah kept her vow that her long-desired child would belong to the Lord.

She put the most treasured thing in her life in God's hands, dedicating her beautiful gift to the One who gave it. We have a powerful example in Hannah's sacrifice. She honored God with what He gave her.

We must ask ourselves: Are we honoring God with what He has given us? Do we dedicate our gifts to Him? Do we place the most beloved things in our lives in His hands?

To be true spiritual warrior women, God should be first in our hearts and in our lives. Nothing should come between us and our Lord. In fact, if Jesus is first in our hearts, then we will be able to honor Him with what He has given us. We will be able to love our husband and children the right way—with His love.

We will be able to keep our careers, hobbies, goals, and all the other aspects of life in their proper places.

Hannah also provides us with a lesson on what God can do when we place things in His hands. He can orchestrate things in magnificent ways—ways we cannot even fathom. Look at what God did with Hannah's sacrifice. Samuel grew up to be one of the greatest prophets in the Old Testament. Not only that, but God blessed Hannah and gave her three more sons and two daughters. You see, God does not take sacrifice like this lightly. He knows what it means to give away something beloved. Considering that, let us strive to be like Hannah and honor God with all He has given us and will give us—our lives, our loves, our thoughts, our actions, and all that we have.

Dear God, thank You for all the precious and beautiful gifts You have given me. Please help me to always honor You with them. I especially thank You for the gift of Your Son, Jesus. I pray for Him to be first in my heart and in my life. In Jesus' Name, Amen.

Priorities and Proper Places for Things in My Life:

_____

_____

_____

_____

_____

Chapter 13

Study: The Queen of Sheba

✧

"...she spoke with him about all that was in her heart."
1 Kings 10:2

The Queen of Sheba was impressive. We read her story in both 1 Kings and 2 Chronicles. Many believe the land where she ruled as queen consisted of modern-day Ethiopia and Yemen. The region was significant and tremendously wealthy. Recent discoveries in Ethiopia describe a vast golden treasure believed to have been hers. We know her treasures were amazing. 1 Kings 10:2 describes what she brought with her to meet King Solomon: "She came to Jerusalem with a very great retinue, with camels that bore spices, very much gold, and precious stones..." Imagine what she had back home! What must her wealth have been to be able to give gifts that impressed King Solomon—the richest king in history! They must have been extraordinary.

We learn in verse 10 that "she gave the king one hundred and twenty talents of gold, spices in great quantity, and precious stones. There never again came such an abundance of spices as the Queen of Sheba gave to King Solomon." I wonder what they were! She also gave Solomon great quantities of almug wood that he used to build steps for the temple, his own house, and had instruments made. Because of this, we can know this gift of wood was also extraordinary. The almug wood would have been of the highest quality and beauty to be used for anything in the temple. Verse 12 tells us, "There never again came such almug wood, nor has the like been seen to this day." On top of all these gifts, I am sure the Queen of Sheba was remarkable and beautiful. When she visited King Solomon, I can only imagine the kind of pomp and circumstance there was to behold—surely greater than anything we have witnessed today.

But beyond the riches and splendor, the reason the queen came to visit Solomon is what is significant here. Of course, in part, she wanted to see for herself if all the rumors of his blessings and grandeur were true. But there was something deeper in her quest. We read in 1 Kings 10: "Now when the Queen of Sheba heard of the fame of Solomon concerning the name of the Lord, she came to test him with hard questions..." The questions she asked Solomon must have been ones of depth and weighty matters. The Bible says, "when she came to Solomon, she spoke with him about all that was in her heart." Because she had heard of his fame "concerning the name of the Lord," she likely had serious topics to discuss with the wisest king on earth. I doubt the queen of Sheba would have gone to all the trouble she did for anything less. We are not told what the questions are that she asked Solomon, but we do know that everything she asked was answered and answered well. In verse three we read: "So Solomon answered all her questions; there was nothing so difficult for the king that he could not explain it to her."

This implies that the Queen of Sheba herself was no slouch when it came to study. She was a successful woman —she was a leader and would have been educated in a wide variety of areas. She knew how to rule—she and the land she ruled was very wealthy. We can assume the Queen of Sheba was probably smart. She would have had to have some significant background knowledge to even ask particular questions and then converse with the wisest king in history. The Queen of Sheba desired wisdom and understanding. What is wonderful here is that she went to the source of wisdom to further her studies—Solomon—because she heard God had blessed him with it. She wanted to see for herself if it was true. In verse seven, the queen tells Solomon, "'It was a true report which I heard in my own land about your words and your wisdom. However I did not believe the words until I came and saw with my own eyes; and indeed the half was not told me. Your wisdom and prosperity exceed the fame of which I heard."

The Queen of Sheba has provided us with the standard

for study. She went to the source of wisdom. Spiritual warrior women must do no less. We must always go to the source of all wisdom and truth as we study—God. Everything we read, hear, and watch should be measured against what the Bible says. The Bible is true. Anything that contradicts what it says is not. We absolutely must check what we allow into our eyes, ears, minds, and hearts if we desire to go deeper with Jesus. Just as Philippians 4:8 says, "...whatsoever things are true, whatsoever things are honorable, whatsoever things are just, whatsoever things are pure, whatsoever things are lovely, whatsoever things are of good report; if there be any virtue, and if there be any praise, think on these things." This means that we must know what does and doesn't meet the parameters of Philippians 4:8. The only way to know this is to know what is in the Bible.

As spiritual warrior women, we need to study the Word of God. II Timothy 2:15 tells us, "Be diligent to present yourself approved to God, a worker who does not need to be ashamed, rightly dividing the word of truth." This applies to all of us—regardless of age, education, status, or anything. One of the most prominent and prosperous women in history took what she had studied to the source of wisdom that God had provided at that time. She shared all that was in her heart and came away astonished with what she learned. Let us continually go to the source of wisdom God has provided for us in Himself and in His word. In Matthew 12:42 Jesus said, "The queen of the South will rise up in judgment with this generation and condemn it, for she came from the ends of the earth to hear the wisdom of Solomon;

and indeed a greater than Solomon is here." We have the greatest source of wisdom there is available to us. Let us go to Jesus and share with Him all that is in our hearts, and we will come away awed and blessed.

Dear God, please help me always come to You as the true source of wisdom. I pray that You would help me pray more, read the Bible more, and understand it better. In Jesus' Name, Amen.

What I Plan to Study in the Bible:

_____

_____

_____

_____

_____

_____

_____

_____

_____

_____

Chapter 14

Resourcefulness: Lydia

❦

"The Lord opened her heart to heed the things spoken by Paul."
Acts 16:14

In Chapter 16 of the Book of Acts, we read of a woman named Lydia. She lived in the city of Philippi, a major city in Macedonia. At that time, Macedonia was a Roman colony and lots of trading for the region would likely have taken place there. Lydia was a seller of purple. This means she most likely sold purple cloth. While purple cloth is rather commonplace today, back then, it was not so easy to come by. We can either run to the store and buy whatever purple thing we want or if we needed to dye something purple, we could grab a box of purple dye and color it. In Lydia's time, purple dye came from a fish and was difficult to obtain. Fabric that was dyed purple would have been quite costly.

The Bible doesn't specify if Lydia simply acquired purple goods and then sold them, or if she created them herself. Either way, we know Lydia was resourceful. She likely knew who to go to when she needed purple dye. Or perhaps she knew which fisherman could supply her with the fish to make the dye herself. At the very least, she would have known the best fabric merchants to supply her successful business. Regardless, Lydia knew how to acquire what was valuable.

When we meet Lydia in Acts 16:14, Paul, Silas, Timothy, and the writer of Acts (traditionally believed to be Luke), had just arrived in Macedonia. In verses 13-14 we read, "And on the Sabbath day we went out of the city to the riverside, where prayer was customarily made; and we sat down and spoke to the women who met there. Now a certain woman named Lydia heard us. She was a seller of purple from the city of Thyatira, who worshiped God. The Lord opened her heart to heed the things spoken by Paul." So, here was a successful businesswoman in a major city in Macedonia, who was serving God—yet she had not heard the Gospel. We know Lydia and her whole household became followers of Jesus. The writer of Acts tells us in verse 15, "And when she and her household were baptized, she begged us, saying, 'If you have judged me to be faithful to the Lord, come to my house and stay.' So she persuaded us."

I imagine as a successful businesswoman, especially in the trade of costly goods, Lydia knew how to bargain. She would know when to speak and when to listen. She would know when to throw in something to seal a deal. I find it interesting that she persuaded Paul, Silas, Timothy, and Luke to stay at her house the way she did. It speaks to her resourcefulness, but also how she recognized the value of the Gospel these men preached. She knew it was priceless. In fact, it appears a church formed and met at Lydia's house. We read in Acts 16 how Paul and Silas were beaten and jailed for casting the spirit of divination out of a slave girl. This is the famous story where Paul and Silas sang praise songs to God and a great earthquake shook the prison, causing the doors to open, yet no one fled. This led to the salvation and baptism of the prison keeper and his family. In verse 40 we read, "So they went out of the prison and entered the house of Lydia; and when they had seen the brethren, they encouraged them and departed."

Lydia's story offers us an important lesson: We cannot truly know what is valuable unless God opens our hearts to heed it. In Acts 16:14 we read: "The Lord opened her heart to heed the things spoken by Paul." This led to Lydia and her household being saved and baptized. Lydia was then able to use all her resources to help establish one of the first churches in Philippi.

In Ephesians 1:18-19 it says, "...having the eyes of your hearts enlightened, that you may know what is the hope to which He has called you, what are the riches of His glorious inheritance in the saints, and what is the immeasurable greatness of His power toward us who believe..." Spiritual warrior women, we need God to open our hearts and help us know this blessed hope and what is truly valuable the way He did for Lydia. How often do we lose sight and become wrapped around the axle of meaningless distractions or worldly goals? Sisters, we don't have to! Lydia was obviously a hard-working woman who ran a successful business. She used her resources to honor God. She was described as a worshiper of God by the writer of the Book of Acts. Lydia understood cost and value and the worth of things. But most importantly, by the grace of God, Lydia was able to recognize the most valuable thing of all—Jesus! May God give us grace and open our hearts so we can heed Him!

Dear God, please open my heart to know You more. Please help me to always recognize what is truly valuable and use all my resources to honor You. In Jesus' Name, Amen.

What is Truly Valuable in My Life:

_____

_____

_____

_____

_____

_____

_____

_____

_____

_____

Chapter 15

Good Works: Tabitha

❧

"Now there was in Joppa a disciple named Tabitha...she was
full of good works and charity." Acts 9:36

When we read about Tabitha in the New Testament, we
are not told much about her; however, her brief story is striking.
She is first described in Acts 9:36: "Now there was in Joppa a
disciple named Tabitha, which translated means [gazelle]."
Perhaps we aren't given more of a description because we don't
need one. In fact, what we are told about Tabitha is really one of
the most honorable descriptions that could be said about
anyone—a disciple. This means she was one of the earliest
Christians—part of the original group of followers of Jesus.
Maybe she met Jesus in person or saw Him speak somewhere.
At minimum, she had become a believer and her testimony was
well known by others.

The rest of verse 36 describes Tabitha this way: "She was full of good works and charity." Wow. Another great and honorable description with important implications. This says something about how she lived her daily life. As a disciple of Jesus, Tabitha, and those who knew of her testimony, understood she was not saved by those good works—that she was saved only through faith in Jesus by the grace of God. Ephesians 2:8-9 tells us, "For by grace you have been saved through faith, and that not of yourselves; it is the gift of God, not of works, lest anyone should boast." What her good works displayed was how Jesus had saved her—they were the outward evidence of an inner transformation. Look at what it says in James 2:14-17: "What good is it, my brothers, if someone says he has faith but does not have works? Can that faith save him? If a brother or sister is poorly clothed and lacking in daily food, and one of you says to them, 'Go in peace, be warmed and filled,' without giving them the things needed for the body, what good is that? So also faith by itself, if it does not have works, is dead." In other words, if Jesus has saved you, then there should be confirmation of that in how you live. Does it mean we will suddenly be perfect? No, of course not! But there should be evidence that we belong to Him. Matthew 5:15-16 says, "Nor do people light a lamp and put it under a basket, but on a stand, and it gives light to all in the house. In the same way, let your light shine before others, so that they may see your good works and give glory to your Father Who is in Heaven." For the writer of Acts to describe Tabitha as he did, she let her light shine as she lived out her faith.

As we read the rest of Tabitha's story, we find in verse 37 that "she became ill and died." The Bible says the disciples sent for Peter (who was nearby) asking him to come right away. After Peter arrived, he went to the room where "All the widows stood beside him weeping and showing tunics and other garments [Tabitha] had made while she was with them" (verse 39). Given everything else we know about Tabitha, I think we can safely assume the garments she made were not for herself—just further evidence of her charity.

Wait! There's more! Verse 40 tells us, "But Peter put them all outside, and knelt down and prayed; and turning to the body he said, 'Tabitha, arise.' And she opened her eyes, and when she saw Peter she sat up." Incredible! But the story doesn't stop there: "And he gave her his hand and raised her up. Then, calling the saints and widows, he presented her alive. And it became known throughout all Joppa, and many believed in the Lord" (verses 41-42). So, God used this kind woman to bless others physically through her good works and charity. But then, He did what only He can do—He took Tabitha's illness, death, return to life, and used it to bring others to the greatest blessing of all—faith in Jesus.

Spiritual Warrior Women, are we like Tabitha—living out our faith every day? Does the word "disciple" accurately describe each of us? Are we known for our good works and charity because we have been transformed by the power of Jesus? As we grow in our relationship with Him, we should be bearing this type of fruit. Colossians 1:10 says we ought to "...walk worthy of the Lord, fully pleasing Him, being fruitful in every good work and increasing in the knowledge of God..." In this way, our lives (and whatever occurs in them) can bear testimony to the beautiful transforming grace of God's love through our Savior, Jesus. Let us make ourselves available to God for Him to use to bring others to the Lord. And may we too, like Tabitha, be honored with the title of disciple, full of good works and charity.

Dear God, please work in my life so that it is evident that I am a follower of Jesus. Please use me to bring others to salvation. May You be honored and glorified in my life every day. In Jesus' Name, Amen.

Evidence God is Working in My Life:

_____

_____

_____

_____

_____

_____

_____

_____

_____

Chapter 16

Humility: Mary of Bethany

"And she had a sister called Mary, who sat at Jesus' feet and listened." Luke 10:39

Mary of Bethany was the sister of Lazarus and Martha. She was the one who sat at Jesus' feet while He was teaching. Martha had met Jesus when He entered their village and she welcomed Him into their home. We read in Luke 10:40 that while Mary was listening to Jesus, "Martha was distracted with much serving, and she approached Him and said, 'Lord, do You not care that my sister has left me to serve alone? Therefore tell her to help me.' And Jesus answered and said to her, "Martha, Martha, you are worried and troubled about many things. But one thing is needed, and Mary has chosen that good part, which will not be taken away from her."

Mary, Martha, and Lazarus not only believed in Jesus, but they were His close friends. When Lazarus became ill, Mary and Martha sent word to Jesus with the message, "Lord, behold, he whom You love is sick" (John 11:3). In verse five it says, "Now Jesus loved Martha and her sister and Lazarus." Can you imagine? Being good friends with Jesus like that when He was here—close enough to send that kind of message and have it written in the Bible specifically that Jesus loved you? Think about this: Mary and Martha *knew* where Jesus was at the time (He was not in their village), so they must have talked before about His travel plans before He left. They had welcomed Jesus into their home. They surely spent a great deal of time together— enough to become close friends.

As Jesus was nearing Bethany, Martha went to meet Him. Lazarus had already died, and the first thing Martha did when she saw Jesus was to say, "Lord if You had been here, my brother would not have died." Jesus then told her that her brother would live again. Martha assumed He was referring to the resurrection at the last day, but Jesus said, "I am the resurrection and the life. He who believes in Me, though he may die, he shall live. And whoever lives and believes in Me shall never die. Do you believe this?" We read in verse 27 that Martha did believe and then she confessed Jesus as "the Christ, the Son of God, who is to come into the world." The Bible doesn't share much on their conversation, but we know Martha secretly sent word to Mary about Jesus' arrival. Her message to Mary was: "The Teacher has come and is calling for you." Then we read in verse

29 that, "As soon as [Mary] heard that, she arose quickly and came to Him."

Now when Mary went to meet Jesus, the first thing she did was to fall at His feet. But, we read in verse 32, that after Mary fell at His feet, she said the exact same thing Martha had said: "Lord, if You had been here, my brother would not have died." It appears that Jesus was moved by Mary's sorrow and the sorrow of those who were with her. Verse 33 tells us, "Therefore, when Jesus saw her weeping, and the Jews who came with her weeping, He groaned in the spirit and was troubled."

As we continue to study this account, we learn, after Jesus told them to roll the stone away, Martha brought up yet another worry—this time about the smell. We don't know what Mary said or did right then, but based on the descriptions we have of her, she wasn't the complaining type, nor one who worried over what others would think. In fact, in every account we have of Mary of Bethany, her actions were full of humility.

The most memorable one that we know of comes from John 12 verses 1-3: "Then six days before the Passover, Jesus came to Bethany, where Lazarus was who had been dead, whom He had raised from the dead. There they made Him a supper; and Martha served, but Lazarus was one of those who sat at the table with Him. Then Mary took a pound of very costly oil of spikenard, anointed the feet of Jesus, and wiped His feet with her hair. And the house was filled with the fragrance of the oil." Although her humble act of love and

85

honor for Jesus brought ridicule from others (consider the source), look at how Jesus responded to her in verse 7: "Let her alone; she has kept this for the day of My burial. For the poor you have with you always, but Me you do not have always." In Matthew's account Jesus also says, "Assuredly, I say to you, wherever this gospel is preached in the whole world, what this woman has done will also be told as a memorial to her."

Every single time we read about Mary of Bethany, she was at the feet of Jesus. In each case, she humbled herself before Him. When she first met Him, she sat at His feet and listened. When He came in response to her and Martha's message concerning Lazarus, she fell at His feet and wept. At a special supper in Jesus's honor, she anointed His feet with oil and wiped them with her hair. Such humility is borne out of a sincere, deep, and reverent love for her Savior. When Mary of Bethany was with Jesus, she didn't seem to notice (or care) if anyone else was around, even if they opposed her or ridiculed her. Notice, too, that each time, Jesus fought for her—when Martha wanted Him to make Mary get up and serve instead of learn, when death threatened to keep her brother in the grave, and when she was scorned for using costly oil to anoint Him before His death on the cross—every time, Jesus blessed and honored Mary. Psalm 149:4 says, "For the Lord takes pleasure in His people; He adorns the humble with salvation."

Spiritual Warrior Women, we need this same humility.

The kind that would cause us to sit at the feet of Jesus and hang on His every word as seen in Mary of Bethany. We need humble hearts so we can fall at His feet when trials and sorrow come, knowing He is enough, no matter what has happened. We should be overflowing with so much love and gratitude for all He has done for us that we bow before Him in humble worship. And like Mary of Bethany, when our Teacher calls to us, let us quickly arise and go to Him.

Dear God, thank You for Your wonderful gift of salvation and eternal life given to me through Jesus. Please help me to serve You with love and humility and to honor You with my whole life. In Jesus' Name, Amen.

What Else the Bible Says About Humility:

_____

_____

_____

_____

_____

_____

_____

_____

_____

_____

Chapter 17

Filled with the Holy Spirit: Elizabeth

"Elizabeth was filled with the Holy Spirit." Luke 1:41

By all accounts, Elizabeth should have been too old to have children. She and her husband Zacharias probably thought they never would, although we know they wanted and prayed for children. The Bible says Elizabeth was barren and they "were both well advanced in years" (Luke 1:7). Verses five and six say Zacharias was a "priest of the division of Abijah" and Elizabeth was a descendant of Aaron. Both she and Zacharias were "righteous before God, walking in all the commandments and ordinances of the Lord blameless."

The account in Luke tells us when Zacharias entered the temple, an angel of the Lord appeared. The angel said to

Zacharias in verses 13-15, "'Do not be afraid, Zacharias, for your prayer is heard; and your wife Elizabeth will bear you a son, and you shall call his name John. And you will have joy and gladness, and many will rejoice at his birth. For he will be great in the sight of the Lord, and shall drink neither wine nor strong drink. He will also be filled with the Holy Spirit, even from his mother's womb." The angel declares in verse 17 that John will "make ready a people prepared for the Lord." But Zacharias didn't believe the angel, and basically said he and his wife were too old. This did not go over well. The angel said to Zacharias: "I am Gabriel, who stands in the presence of God, and was sent to speak to you and bring you these glad tidings. But behold, you will be mute and not able to speak until the day these things take place, because you did not believe my words which will be fulfilled in their own time."

That is exactly what happened. Zacharias was mute until everything took place just as Gabriel said. When we read further in verses 36 and 37 of the first chapter of Luke, it is the same angel, Gabriel, who said to Mary that her relative, Elizabeth "has also conceived a son in her old age; and this is now the sixth month for her who was called barren. For with God nothing will be impossible." Sometime after, Mary went to visit Elizabeth. We read in verse 41 that "when Elizabeth heard the greeting of Mary, that the babe leaped in her womb; and Elizabeth was filled with the Holy Spirit." Then in verses 42-45 we read how she spoke a blessing and prophesied over Mary saying, "Blessed is she who believed, for there will be a fulfillment of those things which were told her from the Lord."

When Elizabeth gave birth to a son, there was great rejoicing and acknowledgment of the Lord's mercy toward Elizabeth. The people wondered what she and Zacharias would call the child. It caused quite a stir when Elizabeth declared his name would be John. Everyone wondered why in the world she would say that when no relative had that name. It was certainly going against custom. We read in verse 62 that they "made signs to his father—what he would have him called. And [Zacharias] asked for a tablet and wrote saying, 'His name is John.'" Everyone was astonished. And then suddenly Zacharias was able to speak again! This caused many people to fear the Lord and wonder about all that had taken place for Zacharias and Elizabeth. The Bible doesn't tell us any more about her, but because we know the rest of John the Baptist's story, we can rest assured Elizabeth faithfully fulfilled her God-given task.

Elizabeth provides an important example for us as spiritual warrior women. First, we read how she was righteous and blameless in serving God. Not many women mentioned in the Bible are given this distinction. Another important fact about Elizabeth is that she is one of a few the Bible specifically says, "was filled with the Holy Spirit."

This is how we need to be as well. Especially if we desire a close relationship with Jesus and fruitful prayer life, we desperately need the Holy Spirit. Romans 8:26 says, "Likewise the Spirit also helps in our weaknesses. For we do not know what we should pray for as we ought, but the Spirit Himself makes intercession for us with groanings which cannot be uttered."

The Holy Spirit works in us to transform us and make us like Jesus. It is His own blamelessness and righteousness He gives to us. Titus 3:5 says, "according to His mercy He saved us, through the washing of regeneration and renewing of the Holy Spirit." Sisters, let us live day by day, walking in the Spirit, worshiping the Lord in spirit and in truth, according to Galatians 5:16 and John 4:24. Then He will enable us to faithfully fulfill His callings upon our lives, the way Elizabeth did. May each of us receive the blessing from Romans 15:13: "Now may the God of hope fill you with all joy and peace in believing, that you may abound in hope by the power of the Holy Spirit."

Dear God, thank You for the life-giving work of the Holy Spirit in me. Thank You for transforming me to be more like Jesus. In Jesus' Name, Amen.

How the Holy Spirit is Working in My Life:

_____

_____

_____

_____

_____

_____

_____

Chapter 18

Love: Jochebed

"When she could hide him no longer, she took for him a basket ...She put the child in it and placed it among the reeds by the river bank." Exodus 2:3

Jochebed. Her name is probably not as familiar to us as others in the Bible, however, she played a key role in God's plan for all of humanity. Jochebed was the mother of Moses. At the time of Moses' birth, the children of Israel had been multiplying greatly in the land of Egypt. This disturbed the pharaoh because he feared what might happen if they rose against him. Exodus 1:12-13 says all of the Egyptians "were in dread of the people of Israel. So they ruthlessly made the people of Israel work as slaves and made their lives bitter with hard service..." On top of that, the pharaoh ordered the midwives to kill any sons born to Hebrew women. The midwives did not follow the pharaoh's order. He further decreed that every son born to the Hebrews be cast into the Nile.

During this time, Jochebed gave birth to a son. She hid him for three months. I cannot imagine what it took to hide a newborn child like that. Every little sound or cry could risk discovery. I imagine Jochebed lived on pins and needles during those three long months. And yet those three months were so short—too short a time to give all the love and care she desired to give her beautiful baby boy. In Exodus 2:3 we read, "When she could hide him no longer, she took for him a basket made of bulrushes and daubed it with bitumen and pitch. She put the child in it and placed it among the reeds by the river bank." Try and imagine what was going through Jochebed's mind as she was preparing the basket. She knew she couldn't keep her son hidden forever, and if he was discovered...well I am sure she tried not to dwell on it. So Jochebed made a heart-breaking decision—yet what else could she do so her son could live? She had to let go and leave him utterly in God's hands.

As difficult as it was, it was the exact right decision. No doubt Jochebed had prayed and prayed. And as only God can do, He answered in a way beyond anything Jochebed probably imagined. The Bible says Moses' sister kept an eye on him from a distance. And who should discover him but the pharaoh's daughter! We read that she "she saw the child, and behold, the baby was crying. She took pity on him and said, 'This is one of the Hebrews' children'" (Exodus 2:6). What happens next is pure genius. Moses' sister approached the pharaoh's daughter and offered to fetch a Hebrew nurse for the child. And who would be a more perfect nurse than the child's own mother! But of course, the baby's sister did not utter a word about that or give away who she was. And as if that wasn't wonderful enough, Pharaoh's daughter hired Jochebed to be the nurse for her very own child.

So Jochebed was blessed with precious years with her boy. The Bible does not say how old Moses was when it was time for him to go live with Pharaoh's daughter as her son, but I have no doubt Jochebed treasured every moment. Because of the unselfish love she had for her son, not only was his life saved, but he grew up to be the one God used to lead the children of Israel out of Egypt and eventually receive the ten commandments.

Jochebed's story reminds us of what love is—it is "patient and kind; love does not envy or boast; it is not arrogant or rude. It does not insist on its own way; it is not irritable or resentful; it does not rejoice at wrongdoing, but rejoices with the truth. Love bears all things, believes all things, hopes all things, endures all things" (1 Corinthians 13:4-7). We need to ask ourselves—is this love evident in our lives? Do we insist on our own way? Do we hope and endure all things?

Do we love unselfishly and sacrificially like Jochebed so others can be saved?

On our own, we cannot. Perfect love comes only from the One who is Love. If we desire to be true spiritual warrior women, we need the love of Jesus. We need to understand the love He has for us, so we can, in turn, love others the way He wants us to. In John 13:34 Jesus said, "A new commandment I give to you, that you love one another; just as I have loved you, you also are to love one another." How did Jesus show His love for us? He gave Himself for us. Romans 5:8 says, "while we were still sinners, Christ died for us." He loves us so much that He was willing to die so we could live with Him forever in Heaven. Because He loved us first, we can love Him (1 John 4:19). And when we love Jesus, we will keep His commandments (John 14:15) and be able to love others with His love—the kind that saves.

Dear God, thank You for Your love for me. Help me to truly love You and to love others so they can come to know You and be saved. In Jesus' Name, Amen.

How I Can Live Out the Love Described in 1 Corinthians 13:4-7:

_____

_____

_____

_____

_____

_____

_____

_____

_____

Chapter 19

Joy: The Five Wise Virgins

❦

"And those who were ready went in with him to the marriage feast, and the door was shut." Matthew 25:10

You've heard of them—in one of Jesus' parables—the wise and foolish virgins. In Matthew 25 we read, "Then the kingdom of Heaven will be like ten virgins who took their lamps and went to meet the bridegroom. Five of them were foolish, and five were wise." The parable tells us they all went to meet the bridegroom, but the five wise virgins took oil with them and the five foolish didn't. It is interesting how in this parable, the bridegroom was delayed, and all ten virgins fell asleep. Then, suddenly, at midnight, he was there! The bridegroom had arrived, and it was time to meet him.

The five wise virgins arose, trimmed their lamps, and were soon ready. The five foolish could not go meet the bridegroom because they had no oil. Not only were the five foolish virgins unprepared, they expected the five wise virgins to give them some of their oil. However, the five wise virgins realized if they gave oil to the foolish virgins, they would be unable to meet the bridegroom. Therefore, they told the foolish virgins to do what they should have done in the first place–go buy their own. The rest of the parable tells us, "And while they were going to buy, the bridegroom came, and those who were ready went in with him to the marriage feast; and the door was shut."

So, the five wise virgins entered into the wedding feast. Throughout the Bible, a wedding (and the wedding feast) are used to represent Heaven. Weddings have always been and continue to be significant times of great joy. They are the beginning of a new beautiful life together and everyone involved shares in the celebration. For Christians, we know God gave us marriage between a man and a woman and that it is a symbol of Jesus and His church. Right now, the bride (who we are–the church) is waiting for the bridegroom, Jesus, to return. We do not know the day or the hour. Jesus makes this important point that Jesus makes many times in His parables. Matthew 25:13 says, "Watch therefore, for you know neither the day nor the hour in which the Son of Man is coming." In Mark 13:32-33 we read, "'But concerning that day or that hour, no one knows, not even the angels in heaven, nor the Son, but only the Father. Be on guard, keep awake. For you do not know when the time will come.'" Luke 12:40 tells us, "'You also must be ready, for the Son of Man is coming at an hour you do not expect.'" Like the five wise virgins, we must be ready.

We must be ready to enter into the wedding celebration—the kingdom of Heaven! So, what will it be like? Jesus called it paradise in Luke 23:43 just before He died on the cross: "Truly, I say to you, today you will be with me in paradise." Think of the most beautiful place you have seen on Earth. Now multiply that measure of beauty by a gazillion and it still won't come anywhere near what awaits us in Heaven. And amidst all that beauty we will have joy everlasting. Wow. It never fades and it never ends. It's forever. There's no more sorrow, no more tears, no more pain, no more heartache, no more suffering, and no more death. Just utter, complete, and pure joy in the presence of our Savior. What a wonderful thing for us to anticipate as we live out our lives, preparing so we are ready.

In the meantime, we have families to care for, jobs to go to, bills to pay, laundry to do, and the list goes on! A wise friend once told me that even in the midst of all of these things, we can experience Heaven here on Earth when we walk closely with Jesus. In John 15:10-11 Jesus said, "'If you keep My commandments, you will abide in My love, just as I have kept My Father's commandments and abide in His love. These things have I spoken to you, that My joy may remain in you, and that your joy may be full.'"

As spiritual warrior women, we need to take a few lessons from the five wise virgins. Let us first, be wise to look forward to our Bridegroom's return. Let us be prepared, having received salvation through faith in Jesus, so that our lamps are already full of oil when we meet Him face to face. And let us follow Jesus, so that our joy may be full here on Earth until we enter in to the wedding celebration and cry out what is written in Revelation 19:6-7, "Hallelujah! For the Lord our God the Almighty reigns. Let us rejoice and exult and give Him the glory, for the marriage of the Lamb has come." Joy!

Dear God, I pray that You would help me walk closely with Jesus every day and that my joy may be full. Please make me ready to meet Him face to face. In Jesus' Name, Amen.

What the Bible Says About Heaven:

_____

_____

_____

_____

_____

_____

_____

_____

_____

Chapter 20

Suit Up: The Armor of God

"Therefore take up the whole armor of God..." Ephesians 6:13

Can you imagine a soldier marching into battle without any gear? How about in a t-shirt and shorts instead of the military-issued combat uniform specifically designed to protect the soldier, that fits perfectly enough for the soldier to engage in combat without hindrance? It seems unthinkable. What if that soldier only took a defensive position? What if the army's strategy was for you to just keep your head down, stay out of sight, and avoid attention? Maybe the enemy will just go away. It's ridiculous sounding, I know. Yet, too often, this is what many Christians do every day. Many don't even realize they are treading on a field of war. For those who do, sadly, they are often ill-equipped, unprepared, and unaware they have been outfitted with the most protective covering and powerful arsenal there is: The Armor of God.

Ephesians 6:10-11 tells us, "Finally, be strong in the Lord and in the strength of His might. Put on the whole armor of God, that you may be able to stand against the schemes of the devil."

Notice that we are told in verse 10 to be strong in the Lord and in the power of His might—not our own strength and not our own power, but the Lord's, because under our own strength and power we are helpless. God knows this. And He understands us. Isaiah 41:10 says, "Fear not, for I am with you; be not dismayed, for I am your God. I will strengthen you, Yes, I will help you, I will uphold you with My righteous right hand." Why would God tell us this? Why is it necessary for Him to remind us not to be afraid and that He will uphold us?

WAR!

We are in a war and we have an enemy. But this war is not a physical one, although we experience its effects. It's spiritual. Ephesians 6:12 spells it out: "For we do not wrestle against flesh and blood, but against principalities, against powers, against the rulers of darkness of this age, against spiritual hosts of wickedness in the heavenly places."

There is a spiritual battle being waged against us and we must fight. We must fight for the eternal salvation of our loved ones. We must fight so the ones we love who are saved will stand firm and strong. We must fight so we can live in a country like the one described by Psalm 33:12: "Blessed is the nation whose God is the Lord." Finally, we must fight for our own priceless walk with Jesus, so one day when, we stand before

102

Him, we can hear the most beautiful words we forever hope to hear: "Well done good and faithful servant...Enter into the joy of your Master" (Matthew 25:21). And until that day comes, we have a mission to fulfill.

Like any good soldier on a critical mission, we must know what equipment we have been issued and we must understand how it works. However, equipment and knowledge mean nothing unless we wear it! So, let's suit up.

Ephesians 6:14 says, "Stand therefore, having fastened on the belt of truth..." Notice here that the belt of truth is already on, then you stand. Spiritual Warrior Women, do you know the Truth? There is only One. It's not about our opinions, or how we think, feel, or anything other than the Word of God. Jesus is the Word. He is the "Truth, the Light, and the Way" (John 14:6). We must know Him to know the Truth. In the rest of John 14:6 Jesus says, "No one comes to the Father except through Me." And like a belt that holds up a pair of battle fatigues, the belt of truth holds our armor together.

Then comes the breastplate of righteousness. This makes me think of a huge piece of armor, thick and heavy, that absolutely nothing can penetrate. A breastplate guards your vital organs, your lungs, and most importantly, your heart. Proverbs 4:23 says, "Keep your heart with all vigilance, for from it flow the springs of life." A breastplate of righteousness guards your heart against evil. Oh, we so desperately need this! Jeremiah 17:9 reminds us that our hearts cannot be trusted: "The heart is deceitful above all things, and desperately sick;

who can understand it?" We know this to be true. That is why to be true spiritual warrior women, we must pray and ask the Lord as it says in Psalm 139:23-24: "Search me, O God, and know my heart! Try me and know my thoughts! And see if there be any grievous way in me, and lead me in the way everlasting!" As we seek the Lord, He is faithful to work in us and purify our hearts. With Jesus as our Savior, we are covered with His righteousness given to us by God "through faith in Jesus Christ to all who believe" (Romans 3:23).

So, we have the belt of truth, the breastplate of righteousness, and now it's time to put on shoes because brave soldiers also march. They follow the general's orders and go where he sends them. Ephesians 6:15 says, "...and, as shoes for your feet, having put on the readiness given by the Gospel of peace." God is telling us to be ready—in fact, that is our main mission—the Great Commission. Wherever He sends us or has us—a faraway country, a new job, our neighborhood, and especially in our own homes—that is our mission field.

Because we are at war, we have an adversary and will face opposition. And when we do, we should neither be shaken nor surprised. After all, Jesus said in John 16:33, "In the world you will have tribulation. But take heart; I have overcome the world." That is why we can "in all circumstances take up the shield of faith, with which [we] can extinguish all the flaming darts of the evil one" (Ephesians 6:16). When we stand behind the protective shield of faith, those darts become quite powerless—especially in light of the One to Whom we belong.

This leads us to the helmet of salvation. Now if you think about helmets, whether worn by athletes or soldiers, they have distinguishing shapes or markings that identify to which team or country they belong. In that same way, when we "take the helmet of salvation," it shows that we belong to Jesus and are in His army! In fact, Ephesians 1:13 says when we "believed in Him, [we] were sealed with the promised Holy Spirit."

And finally, our armor includes a weapon—which means we have something we are supposed to wield. That weapon is the "sword of the Spirit, which is the Word of God" (Ephesians 6:17). The way we wield it is spelled out in verse 18: "praying at all times in the Spirit, with all prayer and supplication."

Spiritual warrior women, when we are fully outfitted in the whole armor of God, there is no reason for us to be fearful or timid. Jesus has given us everything we need as we fight "against principalities, against powers, against the rulers of the darkness of this age, against spiritual hosts of wickedness in heavenly places." And when the battle is won—and praise God we know it will be—we will stand with Him in victory. So, what are we waiting for? It's time to suit up!

Dear God, thank You for Your wonderful provision. Help me to put on and use the full armor You have given me. In Jesus' Name, Amen.

My Prayer List:

Part 2

Wielding Your Weapons

Chapter 21

Commit to Prayer
with Amanda Mc Candless

"My King and my God, for to You I will pray. My voice You shall hear in the morning, O Lord; In the morning I will direct it to You, and I will look up." Psalm 5:2-3

Ahh, I was finally relaxed, ready to spend my quiet time. I had my comfy chair, devotional, prayer journal, cool colorful pens and my coffee. I was excited to hear from the Lord. Instead, I heard intense screaming, yelling, and crying. It sounded like World War III just broke out in the living room.

The war began over kid #2 being on kid #1's side of the couch! I found myself in extreme anger. All I wanted to do was have a quiet time. I needed it. I was frustrated. I needed to be recharged. I needed direction. Just as I needed that alone quiet time, I had two children who needed me. I took a couple of deep breaths to keep from losing it and prayed internally: "Lord help me." I began to cry, "Lord I just want time with You."

Spiritual warrior women, have you been there or somewhere similar—feeling like you don't even have time to think let alone spend time in prayer?

As I cried, I felt the Lord comfort me and that He understood the stage of life I was in. It was time to help my children. And in that instance, I realized the Lord wasn't there pointing His finger at me with an angry face. He didn't have a stopwatch in His hand counting the minutes that I prayed. God's understanding gave me great comfort, but it wasn't a cop-out, either. I knew I needed to make time to meet with Him, somehow, someway.

If we want to be true spiritual warrior women, if we want to follow God—I mean seriously-walking-in-the-Spirit following God, then time with Him is a non-negotiable. There is no other way.

For the past several years of my life, it has been a priority to consistently have alone time with the Lord. But before that, I wasn't disciplined. I viewed my time with the Lord as something that could be skipped. I thought things like, "the Lord will be understanding," (and He always is), I can pray in the car (of course), God knows what I need (He does!), and so on. All true statements, and God is graceful, but none of that should be an excuse for not committing to spending quality time with Him.

It wasn't until I began viewing my quiet time or devotional time as that non-negotiable, that my relationship with God began to soar. (Funny how that works!) I told myself, "You have to do it. Just as I would not leave the house without brushing my teeth or leave the house without clothes." This commitment is what it took for me to have a consistent time of prayer. And when I look back, it was a significant turning point for the better in my prayer life, which spilled over into my everyday life—which is spilling over into my children's lives! The Bible tells us in Colossians 4:2 to "Continue steadfastly in prayer, being watchful in it with thanksgiving." When we read about Jesus' life, we see how common it was for Him to go off alone and pray. How much more do *we* need it then?! Especially when our schedules are so full. We don't have the time to not pray. We don't have the strength to not pray. In Psalm 5:2-3 it says, "My King and my God, for to You I will pray. My voice You shall hear in the morning, O Lord; In the morning I will direct it to You, and I will look up."

If anyone has ever accomplished anything in life it took discipline and determination. For someone to lose weight they must get serious about it—taking all measures to make it happen. Getting serious about my daily devotional time with my Lord and Savior took me adopting the attitude that it was just as important as brushing my teeth every morning. And really, it is vastly more important! But that commitment to prayer has made the difference.

Life is hard. No matter what phase of life we are in, times get difficult. So, we must carve out a quiet time. It doesn't have to be perfect, just sincere. Just us and Jesus. And don't think that once we commit there will be no distractions or interruptions. We know they will come but that's OK. Through God's strength we will keep pushing on. Our children (whether they are little, middle, or grown) are learning how to be warriors from watching us be faithful in prayer and regard that time as of the utmost importance. In fact, we can't do anything else that accomplishes more in our days. May we stay strong and be warriors for our time with God. For our own sakes and our families, let us commit to pray.

It's been nearly eight years since that World War III incident and I'm fighting to keep that time consistent. The demands of life and especially as a mom can make it feel like a battle, but that specific time with the Lord is worth it. He'll do more through that time than anything else I could set out to do, so I will keep at it. I am reminded of Jeremiah 33:3 when the Lord says, "'Call to Me, and I will answer you, and show you great and mighty things, which you do not know.'" Spiritual warrior women, let us take God up on His offer! Let us call upon Him every day, so as Paul said in Galatians 6:9, we will "...not lose heart in doing good." Let us commit to meeting daily with God.

Dear God, please help me commit to pray and stick to that commitment. Please help me not lose heart in doing good. In Jesus' Name, Amen.

My Commitment to Pray:

_____

_____

_____

_____

_____

_____

_____

_____

_____

_____

Chapter 22

Be Available to God
with Pat Self

❧

"Also I heard the voice of the Lord saying: 'Whom shall I send, and who will go for Us?' Then I said, "Here am I! Send me."
Isaiah 6:8

My husband was the one who led me to Christ. He taught me what it means to be a Christian. Not long after he led me to the Lord, he died.

That was 50 years ago.

After my husband went to be with Jesus, I continued in the ministry God had given us. Since that time, I have spent my life simply being available to God. That means that I go where He sends me when He sends me. It sounds easier on paper than it is in real life.

My daughter was ten years old when her daddy passed away. As a single mom, I did my utmost to raise her to know and walk with Jesus. I lived out my faith in front of her, day by day. Let me tell you—I lived on faith. My sole income was from our ministry. It was completely dependent on others' generosity, but in reality, it was dependent upon God's provision. And He provided!

For 40 years, I lived in Connecticut and then Virginia. I ministered to all those God brought my way. Most of the time, someone needed wise counsel, prayer, or a friendly ear to listen. Then God called me to a foreign land—Texas.

All I could say, was "Yes." After all, I truly believed God was sending me, and it was where my husband grew up. So, my daughter (now a single mother herself), my granddaughter, and I went.

Life in Texas has been challenging, rewarding, and the most exciting season of life to date, and I am nearing my eighth decade! God has enabled me to continue in ministry, scheduling what I like to call "divine appointments" on a near-daily basis.

Over the years, I have learned how important it is for Christians to "die to self." Jesus said in Luke 9:23-24, "If anyone desires to come after Me, let him deny himself, and take up his cross daily, and follow Me. For whoever desires to save his life will lose it, but whoever loses his life for My sake will save it." Spiritual warrior women, our lives are not our own. We were bought with a price (1 Corinthians 6:20).

116

I have found that when you obey God and follow Him, you begin to live with purpose. He gives us fresh starts and clean slates. When we fully yield to the Lord, He takes over and does amazing things. He gives "beauty for ashes, the oil of joy for mourning, the garment of praise for the spirit of heaviness; that they may be called trees of righteousness, the planting of the Lord, that He may be glorified" (Isaiah 61:3).

Friends, He does it all! We may be weak, but God is strong. All we need to be is willing. Or maybe your prayer is: "I am willing to be willing." Go to God in sincerity and He will respond. In Psalm 51:17 we read, "...A broken and a contrite heart—these, O God, You will not despise."

For many years now, I have talked to Jesus as a friend. It makes a world of difference to realize Jesus truly is your friend. In fact, He is the best friend we could ever have. He laid down His life for us, and there is no greater love than that! (John 15:13). He even calls us friends: "...but I have called you friends, for all things that I heard from My Father I have made known to you" (John 15:15). He makes Himself available to us every minute of every day of every year without fail and I have been astounded watching what He can do when I am willing and available to Him.

Spiritual warrior women, if we want God to use us, let's make ourselves available. Keep in constant connection with Him throughout the day—no matter how hectic or slow it may be—keep an ear out for that still small voice. "My sheep hear My voice, and I know them and they follow Me" (John 10:27).

117

I am reminded of Isaiah 6:8: "Also I heard the voice of the Lord saying: 'Whom shall I send, and who will go for Us?' Then I said, "Here am I! Send me." I said that to the Lord many years ago. My life has been and still is a wonderful adventure. I am eternally thankful for the journey He has called me on. He has shown Himself faithful through joy, pain, ease, difficulty, abundance, and scarcity. He will do the same for you.

Be available to God and see for yourself.

Dear God, I am willing to be available to You. Please help me hear Your voice and follow You wherever You lead me. In Jesus' Name, Amen.

How God Has Shown Himself Faithful in My Life:

_____

_____

_____

_____

_____

_____

_____

_____

_____

Chapter 23

Abide in Worship

with Misha Goetz

❧

"...be filled with the Spirit, speaking to one another in psalms and hymns and spiritual songs, singing and making melody in your heart to the Lord, giving thanks always for all things to God the Father in the name of our Lord Jesus Christ."
Ephesians 5:18-20

Eyes open. I breathe in. It's another day. My thoughts go to the dishes in the sink, the toys on the floor, the unfinished to-do list from yesterday. Another moment passes before I lift my head—another moment passes, and I breathe in again. It is at this moment, in the passing breaths of the early morning that I am faced with a choice. How am I to live—today? The Bible tell us in Matthew 6:34, "So do not worry about tomorrow; for tomorrow will care for itself. Each day has enough trouble of its own" (NASB). Jesus, or Yeshua, as I grew up calling Him in my Messianic Jewish household, spoke these words to his disciples and He speaks these words to us. "For He knows our frame; He remembers that we are but dust" (Psalm 103:14). He knows every thought before it comes, He knows every fear that has yet to appear. He knows we are fragile, and He knows we need to be reminded, each and every day, moment by moment, of His ever-present presence. That is why, in the passing breaths of the early morning, I choose to get up, get out of bed, and find a quiet place to commune with Adonai (Hebrew for 'the Lord').

I am a wife, a mom, a daughter, a worship leader, a songwriter, a producer, a booking agent, and many other things on a daily basis—but first and foremost, I am a daughter of the King. It is in this place of sitting and listening before the King that I find my solace, my peace, and my strength to face today. I try, each and every day, to open my Bible and read. It is in the early hours of the morning that I find the time to sit in the quiet and soak in His wonderful Word, for "Man shall not live by bread alone, but by every word that proceeds from the mouth of God" (Matthew 4:4). Those sweet morning times are my daily bread, and I cherish them. There are days, though, when I hit the snooze. There are days when my three-year-old son comes into my room extra early, and there are days I just need more sleep. On those days, prayer and worship mean more to me than ever. In fact, having a good morning devotional time isn't the golden ticket to a perfect day, but it is what helps me abide in His presence throughout it. And it is only by His Spirit that I "live and move and have [my] being" (Acts 17:28). By His Spirit, He goes with me throughout the day, and gives me life. By His Spirit, moment by moment, He sustains me as I drop my son off at school and head to work. The beautiful thing is that I have access to His Spirit every moment of every day. It is through prayer and worship that I commune with the One I so desperately need.

It is easy to get caught up. It is so easy to think about ourselves and our to-do lists, because there is simply so much that must be done! It is so easy to go mindlessly scrolling through social media, and it is so easy to fly on autopilot just to get through the day. Yet, that's not the life we've been called to. Spiritual warrior women, we have been called to "pray without ceasing" and "in everything give thanks" (1 Thessalonians 5:17,18). It is in a posture of perpetual praise that we are meant to live. Ephesians 5:19-20 tells each of us to be "filled with Spirit, speaking to one another in psalms and hymns and spiritual songs, singing and making melody in your heart to the Lord, giving thanks always for all things to God the Father in the name of our Lord Jesus Christ." And this is the good life. This is the full life. It only takes a moment, and then another moment, and then another moment.

Worship and prayer are not just what happens on stage week after week, or before bed at night. A life of worship and prayer is summed up in this one word—abide. In the car with our children on the way to school or when we are alone on the way to work, we can lift our voices in praise, with or without a melody, thanking God for the good things He's given. When we're home washing the dishes, we can talk to the Lord about our worries, our fears, our intentions. Like it says in Romans 12:1, we can present our bodies as living sacrifices—holy and pleasing to God throughout the day. Spiritual warrior women, He wants to be involved beyond our morning devotional time. He wants to be involved in our every moment of our every day. When we remember this, and we take the time to attune our ears to His Spirit, and not to ourselves, we can commune, we can abide, and we can worship.

Dear God, please help me to abide in worship in every moment of every day. Please put a song in my heart and a spring in my step and let me praise You. Thank You for everything You have given me. In Jesus' Name, Amen.

My Favorite Verses from Psalms that Worship the Lord:

_____

_____

_____

_____

_____

_____

_____

_____

Chapter 24

Unwrap Your Gift

with Shelly Wilson

"Eye has not seen, nor ear heard, nor have entered into the heart of man, the things which God has prepared for those who love Him." 1 Corinthians 2:9

Have you ever received a beautifully wrapped gift? Do you ooh and ahh over how lovely it is and then set it on a shelf? No! You open it! Whether you rip into the ribbons and paper or carefully undo each part, you **DO** open it. You also read the note that accompanies the gift so not only do you know who gave it to you, you know what they had in mind in giving it.

Hidden within you is a gift from the Lord. James 1:17 says, "Every good gift and every perfect gift is from above, and comes down from the Father of lights, with whom there is no shadow of turning." His very hands tucked away in you details, attributes, and personality traits He knew would come in handy for your divine assignment while on Earth. Woven into the very fiber of your being are His dreams for your life, just like it says in Jeremiah 29:11: "For I know the plans I have for you, declares the Lord, plans for welfare and not for evil, to give you a future and a hope." What a shame if the gift to you, from the Giver of all good gifts, goes unwrapped.

Sadly, many Christians wander aimlessly. They are discouraged and sad. They seem to have no idea who they really are in Christ Jesus. Many who belong to Jesus, for one reason or another, have gifts that remained unopened. This is not how the Body of Christ is supposed to be. The Church in Acts knew the gifts of one another and "employed" them daily for the Kingdom. Dear Christian, you are critical to the mobilization of the army of Christ. You must fulfill your ministry. You are not insignificant. On the contrary, you may be a missing puzzle piece to the greatest war that shall ever be fought.

We can rejoice in the birth of Christ, the crucifixion of Christ, and even the resurrection of Christ and fail to understand there is still more. Salvation is not the end. It is merely the beginning. The "more" moves us past the cross and into the abundant life promised us as we follow Jesus. To be a Christ follower presupposes we are going somewhere with Him. So where is He taking you? I can tell you this much; it will be nothing short of supernatural should you choose to grab His hand and go.

You can be certain the dreams and gifts sown into you by God are meant to be used for His glory. 1 Peter 4:10 says, "As each has received a gift, use it to serve one another, as good stewards of God's varied grace...in order that in everything God may be glorified through Jesus Christ." And the beautiful thing is, you don't have to figure out what your gifts are. It is not necessary to apply a formula or go through a step-by-step plan to determine the gifts God has given you. No, spiritual warrior women, all you have to do is seek the Lord. He will reveal His plans for your life. Ephesians 2:10 tells us, "For we are His workmanship, created in Christ Jesus for good works, which God prepared beforehand, that we should walk in them."

All seasons of life, especially the stormy ones, are training grounds. A training ground is where a warrior goes to get in shape, learn fighting skills and strategies, and gain wisdom and experience for the next battle. To adequately prepare a warrior, the training ground regimen must be intense. This is not unlike the deepest valleys of our lives. In Hosea 2:14-15, we read of unseen "vineyards" that rise from the Valley of Achor, or trouble: "I will give her vineyards from there, and the Valley of Achor as a door of hope." I am convinced your deepest valley will yield your greatest victory in the Kingdom of God. For this is the most intimate place where we can learn the vast gentleness of the Lord's heart toward the broken-hearted and at the same time, emerge on the other side with hard-earned wisdom and a more solid faith. Some gifts are

125

those that could only have sprouted from a difficult season. They cause our hearts to be found most tender to a hurting world in need of what we have learned from a lovely Savior.

As we follow after Jesus, some of our gifts will be easily recognized. Others will be a surprise only Christ Himself knew was in us. He will reveal them according to His perfect plan. Trust God. Remember Romans 8:28: "And we know that for those who love God all things work together for good, for those who are called according to His purpose." Know that His intent is far greater than you could ever think or imagine. 1 Corinthians 2:9 promises, "Eye has not seen, nor ear heard, nor have entered into the heart of man, the things which God has prepared for those who love Him." He is a God of grand adventures. So please, do let Him unwrap your gift.

Dear God, thank You that You have given me gifts. I pray You will bring them to fruition and that they will honor and glorify You. Please help me follow after You so that what You have planned for my life can unfold like the opening of a gift. I want to follow You on the grand adventure You have for me. In Jesus' Name, Amen.

God's Promises to Me:

_____

_____

_____

_____

Chapter 25

Be Bold

with Dana Crosby

❦

"Have I not commanded you? Be strong and courageous. Do not be afraid or discouraged, for the Lord your God will be with you wherever you go." Joshua 1:9

Dictionary.com defines the word "bold" as not hesitating or fearful in the face of actual or possible danger or rebuff; courageous and daring. Are you naturally bold? Some people are. I am not one of those people. Oh, I have strong opinions about things, but, in my flesh, I've been afraid of what other people might think of me. I would keep quiet about my opinions until I knew if it was "safe" to be transparent with someone. Honestly, my pride was afraid that other people would find out what I perceived to be the most dreadful thing in the world: I'm not perfect. I used to live in a prison of fear.

Ever since I was a child, I knew God had a calling on my life to share the Word of God with others. As a teenager, I preached countless bold sermons to my bathroom mirror. I could envision the crowds of people as I beaconed them to repent and turn to Jesus. But one thing continued to blockade my aspirations to honor God with my speech: fear. Not just any fear, fear of the opinions of man. Can you relate? Has fear of what others might think ever inhibited your daydreams of using your gifts for God or following His calling on your life? Can I ask you something? If you could do one thing for Jesus, without any fear of man, or fear of failure, what would it be?

In Chapters 3 and 4 of Exodus, we read of the burning bush encounter between God and Moses. God revealed Himself to Moses and spoke to him on Holy ground. It was there, in grand fashion, that God unveiled His divine rescue plan for His people. As I read the verses, I can almost hear the epic symphony build to a crescendo as God detailed the supernatural redemptive storyline. God highlighted His message of deliverance not with PowerPoint images, but with live snakes and leprosy appearing and disappearing in an instant. Moses was told he would be able to perform miracles on command, and you can almost hear the pregnant pause as the Lord awaited cheers, a fist pump, or perhaps a hearty "Amen!" However, Moses' response was like the sound of crickets. It was totally out of place.

Instead of focusing on what God had promised to do, he focused on his own weaknesses. Whether Moses was truly afraid, or just looking for a reason to bow out, Moses' response shifted the focus from the almightiness of God to himself and the weakness of mankind. And everything about it seems wrong—yet sadly, all too familiar. Moses said to God, "Oh my Lord, please send someone else" (Exodus 4:13, NIV). It's hard to imagine Moses actually saying that directly to God, but he did. And too often, we do it, too. Has God ever given you a vision for which you provided a plethora of reasons as to why it would never work? Many times, we make excuses for not obeying God, or at least, delaying our obedience.

As we continue reading in verse 14, we read that "the Lord's anger burned against Moses..." God did not waste time, either, He gave the honor to someone else—Moses' brother, Aaron. But wasn't just Moses assessing his own strengths and weaknesses? Of course, he had some of both, but that wasn't the point. Moses' focus was on himself—not on God and what He was going to do.

As we walk with the Lord, we become very aware of our shortcomings. However, God delights in using the weak things of this world to display His glory. This is why He reduced the size of Gideon's army. This is why He used a young boy's take-out to feed thousands of people. This is why, in 1 Corinthians 1:27-29 it says, "But God chose the foolish things of the world to shame the wise; God chose the weak things of the world to shame the strong. God chose the lowly things of this world and the despised

131

things—and the things that are not—to nullify the things that are, so that no one may boast before Him" (NIV). He wants His glory and majesty to shine through us so it will be very apparent to those observing that it's not us, it's Him.

In spite of ourselves, our shortcomings, and our strengths, God wants to use us. He wants us to be bold for Him, but not in our own strength or power. Remember Peter? He was so zealous to fight for Jesus that he cut off the ear of the high priest's servant, but turned right around and denied Jesus three times. Peter could not be bold on his own. Zechariah 4:6 tells us, "...'Not by might, nor by power, but by my Spirit,' says the Lord Almighty" (NIV). It wasn't until Peter was filled with the Holy Spirit that he was able to boldly preach, teach, and call those listening to repent.

Spiritual warrior women, we too are called to be bold for Jesus—to share the Good News and be lights shining in a dark world. But we cannot possibly do this on our own. We need the power of the Holy Spirit. That is the only way we can lay aside our pride, our reputations, our strengths, our weaknesses, and all of ourselves, to keep our eyes fixed on Jesus and boldly obey Him. When we are willing to let all of that go, we will walk in a freedom we have never known. When we are focused on Him and Him alone, there is no limit to what God can do with us and through us; nothing can hold us back from doing whatever the Lord asks of us, because He will be with us wherever we go.

Dear God, please set me free from any fears keeping me from living out my purpose in You. Give me the vision You have for my life. Help me walk out the calling You have for me. I will give you my small loaves of bread and my few fish. Please multiply my gifts to serve Your people. In Jesus' Name, Amen.

Areas of My Life Where God Wants Me to Be Bold:

_____

_____

_____

_____

_____

_____

_____

_____

_____

_____

Going Deeper

Be Obedient

with Beckie Lindsey

"For the eyes of the Lord run to and fro throughout the whole earth to show Himself strong on behalf of those whose heart is loyal to Him." 2 Chronicles 16:9

Christians have an arsenal of spiritual weapons at our disposal. Some of the biggies include prayer, faith, praise, and worship. But dare I say, there is one the devil fears most. What is this weapon? The greatest weapon a Christian has against the devil's kingdom is obedience to the Lord. Obedience is what God desires and what Satan fears most. 1 Samuel 15:22 describes the value of obedience: "Does the Lord delight in burnt offerings and sacrifices as much as in obeying the Lord? To obey is better than sacrifice, and to heed is better than the fat of rams" (NIV).

When studying the book of Ruth, we see a theme of faithfulness woven throughout. Obedience should be a natural byproduct of faith. In other words, obedience is "fleshed out faith." The fact that Ruth's story takes place during a time when "...there was no king in Israel; everyone did what was right in his own eyes" (Judges 17:6, NKJV) makes the faithful obedience to God all the more astounding.

The Hebrew word for "obey" in Scripture is **shama** and it means "to hear with attention or interest, to listen, to hear anything that can be perceived by the ear, to obey." The Greek word for "obedience" is hupakoe (from hupó = by, under + akoúo = hear) and means to "hear under," which denotes listening and submitting to that which is heard. This implies that a response to what's being heard often involves a change of attitude in the hearer. We must listen to God's commands in order to obey them. And God is always speaking. But are we always listening? Let's face it, human beings are easily distracted and confused.

Doesn't it make sense that a tactic of the devil would be to influence *if* and *what* we hear? Satan is after our faith and the obedience that follows. For the non-Christian, Satan strives to prevent the listener from truly hearing and putting faith in Jesus. Because we know from Romans 10:17, "So faith

comes from hearing, and hearing through the Word of Christ"
(ESV). For the Christian, one of the main ways Satan weakens
and prevents our faith from growing into obedience is through
deception. The devil's nature is falsehood. He is the liar and
father of lies. He is a master at twisting the truth (John 8:44,
Genesis 3:1). Look at the way the serpent twists God's words
when speaking to Eve in Genesis 3:1: "Did God actually say, 'You
shall not eat of any tree in the garden?'"

Satan uses the same tactic with us in hopes to twist God's
precepts. "The Bible doesn't say there is anything wrong with
pornography." "There's nothing wrong with a little white lie." "I
don't really need to tell the clerk she gave me too much change."
It is of utmost importance to truly hear God's words in order to
put them into the practice of obedience.

If we are not familiar with God's word, we leave ourselves
open to deception which will most likely lead to disobedience.
Even if we are familiar with scripture, our weaknesses make us
susceptible to letting our guard down and obeying the flesh
which leaves us open for further attack from the enemy.

Obedience is protection. But how can we tighten our
resolve to strengthen faithful obedience? How does it look in the
day-to-day life for a believer? Simply stated: It begins with love.
Love the Lord and spend lots of time learning the truths of His
word and applying those truths to your life. Deuteronomy 6:4-9
tells us, "Listen (shama), O Israel! The LORD is our God,
the LORD alone. And you must love the LORD your God with all
your heart, all your soul, and all your strength. And you must

commit yourselves wholeheartedly to these commands that I am giving you today. Repeat them again and again to your children. Talk about them when you are at home and when you are on the road, when you are going to bed and when you are getting up. Tie them to your hands and wear them on your forehead as reminders. Write them on the doorposts of your house and on your gates" (Deuteronomy 6:4-9, NLT).

At first glance, this command seems impossible to obey. In man's natural, sinful state, it is impossible. But the good news is, Christians have been cleansed from sin and have the Holy Spirit to make the impossible possible. Throughout Scripture, the believer's relationship with God is compared to that of a marriage—the most intimate of all relationships. In the passage above, we see that God desires all from us. How do we develop an intimate, love relationship with God?

How to Love God

Love God with all your heart. Love grows over time. I remember telling the Lord, "I know I don't love you with my all. Please help me." This wasn't anything He didn't already know. And God is always faithful. He gives us the desire and the power to do what pleases Him (Philippians 2:13). Love God with all your heart by making Him number one. We prioritize things we care about most. This means reserving the best of your affection for Him. Make time each day to build an intimate relationship with Him through prayer. He wants to know you and be known by you. Let Him speak to you. God's primary way of speaking to us is through the Bible.

Love God with all your soul. In the Old Testament, the "soul" refers to one's whole being. Loving God with all your soul means dedicating your life to Him. We give over our passions, thoughts, and goals to the Lord. We ask Him to guide us in our speech, our careers, our talents, in all our relationships—our entire being should display our love for God. Find out what God values and stay true to those things.

Love God with all your mind. Loving God with our minds means supporting our passion with knowledge. God wants us to use our minds. He does not expect us to have blind faith. Hebrews 11:1 explains, "Now faith is confidence in what we hope for and assurance about what we do not see" (Hebrews 11:1, NIV). There are two aspects of faith: intellectual assent and trust. Intellectual assent means believing something to be true. Trust is actually relying on the fact that something is true.

The Greek word for faith is ***pistis***, which means trust or trustworthy. If you tell someone you have faith in them, you are saying two things. First, you are sure the person actually exists. And secondly, you are convinced the person is trustworthy. We begin to love God with all our minds by asking questions. God is not intimidated or offended by our questions. Read the Bible to find out what words mean. Listen to your pastor and the experiences of others. Take classes. Ask the Lord for guidance. Finally, loving God with all your mind means directing your thoughts to the things He values and allowing Him to transform the way you think (Philippians 4:8, Romans 12:1-3).

Love God with all your strength. Loving God with all our strength means persevering and training each day. The apostle Paul refers to our daily Christian lives as a race to be run with endurance. "Do you not know that in a race all the runners run, but only one gets the prize? Run in such a way as to get the prize. Everyone who competes in the games goes into strict training. They do it to get a crown that will not last, but we do it to get a crown that will last forever.

Therefore I do not run like someone running aimlessly; I do not fight like a boxer beating the air. No, I strike a blow to my body and make it my slave so that after I have preached to others, I myself will not be disqualified for the prize" (1 Corinthians 9:24-27, NIV).

We must be willing to fight with all our strength each day for our relationship with God. True obedience results in intimacy with God. Intimacy promotes love. Love inspires obedience. Jesus says in John 14:15, "If you love Me, obey My commandments" (NLT). When we obey God, we are speaking His love language.

Love covers a multitude of sins, thereby protecting us from Satan's most vicious weapon of disobedience.

As we learned in Ruth's earlier chapter, her story is an example of faithful obedience even in the little things which led to blessings for generations to come. Ruth had no idea the impact her obedience would have. She was just an ordinary person like you and me. But God is in the business of using ordinary people to do extraordinary things. He looks for those who are faithful and obedient and blesses their socks off! "For the eyes of the Lord run to and fro throughout the whole earth to show Himself strong on behalf of those whose heart is loyal to Him." (2 Chronicles 16:9). Being fully committed doesn't mean perfect. That is another trap of the enemy. God is not after perfection— He is after persistence. Like Ruth, Naomi and Boaz, may we persevere to love God with our faithful obedience.

Chapter 26

Put Jesus First in Your Marriage with Dr. Angela Ruark

"I am my beloved's, and my beloved is mine."
Song of Solomon 6:3

My husband and I have been married for almost three decades. I like to say we are still on our honeymoon but we're past the awkward stage. And frankly, it's true. We grow more in love every day. A lot of people have asked us what the secret is to a successful marriage. The secret is not really a secret. Jesus comes first. Period. My husband loves Jesus more than he loves me, and I love Jesus more than I love my husband.

This is the game changer. When a husband and wife each love Jesus first in their lives, suddenly, "self" is out of the picture. The Lord takes the top spot, then the other. Let me tell you, it's

143

the perfect recipe for two imperfect people. As we have shared with many young couples, if you love Jesus first, then He helps you love each other the right way. Of course, this is how God planned it from the beginning. "Therefore a man shall leave his father and mother and be joined to his wife, and they shall become one flesh" (Genesis 2:24). As the husband and wife each seek the Lord individually and together, they grow closer to God and each other.

Praying together every day and for one another is vital—it's a continual breath of life infused into a marriage. Jesus promised to be there when two or more are gathered in His Name (Matthew 18:20). When a husband and wife meet with Jesus every day, they can't help but grow closer to Him and to each other. Over the years, my husband and I have made it a priority. We also pray for each other during the day. Sometimes it's on our own, and sometimes we call each other and pray over the phone, text message, and email.

When you pray together regularly, forgiveness is easy. And forgiveness is crucial in a Godly marriage. We should forgive quickly and permanently. Grudges don't work. The enemy would like nothing better than to drive a wedge between a husband and wife. We should not give that ground. Jesus says in Mark 11:25-26, "And whenever you stand praying, forgive, if you have anything against anyone, so that your Father also Who is in heaven may forgive you your trespasses" (ESV).

Marriage is something that God honors. Therefore, we, too, must honor it. Scripture tells us in Hebrews 13:4, "Let

144

marriage be held in honor among all..." (ESV). This means we must also guard our marriages. Today's culture does the absolute opposite. Have you ever noticed how many TV shows and movies make fun of husbands? Wives in TV shows and movies continually gripe about them and put them down. This is completely contrary to how God would have spiritual warrior women refer to and treat their husbands (Ephesians 5:33). To complain about a husband allows room for the enemy to cause division and it is a mistreatment of your very own flesh and blood, your love, your God-given best friend. Imagine the impact and blessing of a marriage that follows Ephesians 4:29: "Let no corrupt word proceed out of your mouth, but what is good for necessary edification, that it may impart grace to the hearers."

Husbands carry a heavy load whether they let on or not. They benefit greatly when their wives pray for them. God put husbands as heads of their families (Ephesians 5:23). Why wouldn't we want to pray for our husbands to have wisdom when they make decisions that impact the whole family?

If you work outside the home, then you understand the daily stress and pressure. When our sons were young, I was able to stay home—I loved it! But when my husband came in from a long day of work, the first thing I did was pounce! Within the first five minutes, I unleashed every thought and idea I had built up over the course of the entire day. No wonder he always needed a nap after work! Once our sons were older, I worked outside the home, and yep. I get the no pouncing thing.

Because our lives can be hectic and stressful, it's important for us as spiritual warrior women to contribute to the love life part of our marriages. Proverbs 18:22 says, "He who finds a wife finds a good thing." May God help us live up to that. I believe laughter and fun play a large role. Over the years, my husband and I have developed so many inside jokes between us that we now speak them in code to one another. (We also made up our own language, but that's for another time.) No matter where we are or what is going on, one of us can just say one "word" and there is so much meaning behind it that we can't help but crack up. Joyful laughter is good medicine (Proverbs 17:22) and it's a fun form of flirting too. "Let your fountain be blessed, and rejoice with the wife of your youth" (Proverbs 5:18). And I think my husband is just as cute now if not cuter than when I first met him—gray hair included—because he has earned his "crown of glory" (Proverbs 16:31). Laughter and romance go hand in hand.

Speaking of romance, the Song of Solomon provides plenty. It is both metaphorical and practical. The verses provide great examples for us to follow to let our husbands know how much they mean to us. The couple described in those verses were best friends and lovers. Best friends and lovers are confidants, they share in each other's interests (surprise your husband with a date to the hardware store to look at tools and see what happens!), and they genuinely care for one another in what they do and say.

146

Because God is the One who invented marriage, He knows what makes it work best. Sisters, let us pray for our husbands and our marriages, for God's blessing, guidance, and favor. It is by His grace that we can say "I am my beloved's and my beloved is mine" (Song of Solomon 6:3).

Dear God, thank You for my husband. Please help us put You first in our lives and in our marriage. May it be filled with joy, love, laughter, romance, forgiveness, grace, and friendship. In Jesus' Name, Amen.

Prayers for My Husband and Our Marriage:

_____

_____

_____

_____

_____

_____

_____

_____

_____

Chapter 27

Intercede for Your Children

with Tamikia Bell

"Behold, children are a heritage from the Lord, the fruit of the womb is a reward." Psalms 127:3

I call it the PRAYER WOMB. Sixty-three and a half months or 240 weeks, or however you chose to calculate it, this is the amount of time my body spent gestating four sons and three daughters over a 14-year period. Pregnancy is undeniably a miraculous and amazing journey. The ability, honor, and responsibility are given to us women. We serve as human incubators. We nurture and carry a life that becomes intricately woven into every part of who we are.

When life begins at fertilization, the mother soon begins to feel it. She experiences numerous changes. They are exciting, wonderful, and sometimes difficult. Throughout her expectation, the mother feels every little twinge and flutter, yet cannot see anything—except her growing belly!

By the time a woman is visibly pregnant—usually about the fifth or sixth month—she has usually experienced shock, awe, denial, excitement, morning after morning of sickness, and countless trips to the ladies' room. She has also experienced several types of hormonal, psychological and physiological changes. The life within her becomes all consuming; impacting her diet, her sleep, where she can and cannot go, and what she can and cannot do. And of course, there are mood swings and weight gain. But she will tell you it is worth every bit.

As a woman who has carried seven children, I had a different experience with each pregnancy. For some of them, the time flew by. For others, it felt like an eternity. However, every time, the nine months, 40 weeks, 270 days and 6480 hours ended when it came time to give birth. Labor is, well, laborious for lack of a better term. The gamut of emotions combined with the levels of pain cannot accurately be described. You have to give birth yourself to truly know. Regardless, the mission is to give birth and bring forth that baby. The wee one you have been nourishing and carrying is depending on you to help them get through the narrow chamber called the birth canal. The instruction is to *PUSH when you feel the pain.* Eventually, you give birth.

This is the same concept I have utilized when praying for all of my children—from before they were born to this present moment. To intercede for her children is a mother's responsibility and also her honor. Scripture tells us in Psalms 127:3, "Behold, children are a heritage from the Lord, the fruit of the womb is a reward." So, what are we mothers to do with these precious gifts from God?

We cover them with prayer—while they are in the womb, while they are tiny and helpless newborns. We cover them with prayer when they are toddlers, when they are potty training—if you have been through this, then you know—and we cover them with prayer as they reach school age. Of course, it doesn't end there. Little by little, the cord attaching them to you grows longer and longer. As they grow, the need for you to intercede for them grows too.

We must also keep in mind that as mothers we can be helicopters, overbearing, too laidback, passive, or controlling worry warts. But we were never called to be any of those things. We were called to be intercessors and prayer warriors—especially for our children. Deuteronomy 11:19 tells us, "You shall teach them to your children, speaking of them when you sit in your house, when you walk by the way, when you lie down, and when you rise up."

Children learn by imitating. Spiritual warrior women, we need to live out our faith in front of our children. Ephesians 5:1 says, "Therefore be imitators of God as dear children." If we live our lives as this verse describes, our children will see that. They will grow up doing the same.

151

Does this mean everything will turn out perfectly? No, unfortunately it doesn't. The reality is our children will have problems, heartaches, and challenges. Some will even stray from the faith. So, while we have them with us—while we have significant influence over them, we should take absolute advantage, remembering the promise of Proverbs 22:6: "Train up a child in the way he should go, and when he is old he will not depart from it." That is a promise we can stand on.

At every stage of their precious lives, we can and should intercede for them. Spiritual warrior women, we need to be steadfast and bold in our approach—never cowering, wavering or doubting. Prayer can sometimes feel laborious and sometimes the pushback is unrelenting. This is when we need to remember the lesson learned when we gave birth to that child: *PUSH when you feel the pain.* But let us push through in full confidence of the promises set before us concerning our children that were grown in the prayer WOMB—not room but WOMB!

Isaiah 54:13 promises, "And all thy children shall be taught of the Lord; and great shall be the peace of thy children" (KJV). We can do our part and "bring them up in the nurture and admonition of the Lord" (Ephesians 6:4), then trust God to finish the good work He began in them. While we do that, we lift them to the Lord in prayer. Sometimes we stand in the gap for them (Ezekiel 2:20) and other times, we must step back, and watch God do what only He can do. Scripture tells us we can trust God. Remember Jeremiah 29:11, "For I know the plans I have for declares the Lord, plans for welfare and not for evil, to give you a future and a hope" (ESV). Those plans go way back before that baby was in the womb. "Before I formed you in the womb I knew you..." (Jeremiah 1:5). After all, God loves our children even beyond what we are able—and we know how great our love for them is.

Dear God, thank You for my beautiful and precious heritage. Please help me to train them up in the way they should go so when they are old, they will not depart. Help me stand in the gap for them and know You have loved them from before You formed them in my womb. I pray they will serve You all of their lives. In Jesus' Name, Amen.

Prayers for My Children:

_____

_____

_____

_____

_____

_____

_____

_____

_____

Chapter 28

Teach Your Children

with Amanda McCandless, Tracy Malone and Dr. Angela Ruark

"Come you children, listen to me; I will teach you the fear of the Lord." Psalms 34:11

Where and how to educate our children is always a weighty decision. Of course, we want to provide our children with the best options we can. Maybe there are several to choose from or maybe there is only one at the moment. Regardless, educating our children is a matter of continual prayer. This holds true for teaching our children to know and obey God as well as learning reading, writing, math, and other subjects.

God placed the responsibility of teaching children on their parents. First and foremost, we are to teach them to fear the Lord. Psalms 34:11 says, "Come you children, listen to me; I will teach you the fear of the Lord." We must teach our precious gifts from God to know and fear Him, because that is the beginning of wisdom, and to know Him is understanding. (Proverbs 9:10). It is up to us to raise our children in the "fear and admonition of the Lord" (Ephesians 6:4). Even with great churches and wonderful youth programs, the charge was given by God to us. At a minimum, we are overseers of what they are taught, responsible for ensuring that it is biblically sound.

This is also the case when our children reach school age. Whether our children attend public school, private school, or homeschool, the education of our children is on our shoulders. God knows where we are and what circumstances dictate, so there is no need to worry over that—but there is always a need to make prayer a priority.

Amanda

Public school. One of the scariest things as a parent is letting your child go to a school where you have little to no influence. You wonder if the teachers will be nice and patient. You wonder how the other children will act and treat your child. Will your child know what to do, have friends, sit alone at lunch, get bullied, and on and on and on.

After dropping my baby off at kindergarten, I went home with my three-year-old and cried. Yes, I did. I reviewed my kindergartener's schedule numerous times. I counted down the time to pick her up. I even drove by at recess. Yes, I am that crazy. I was first in that car pickup line.

My oldest daughter and I were hardly ever apart. I was a stay-at-home mom for five years. My babysitting list was short—family and one friend. I was always around to protect her and shape her. Now, a teacher whom I met only once was going to take care of my baby. Through a series of events, a ministry change for my husband, a four-hour move, and an income change, I had to return to work. Homeschool or private school just wasn't an option.

Fear set in. Lord what will I do? God reminded me, "I am the parent here." I was shocked. But the more I let it set in, I realized it was true, and my child had the best parent ever. I only thought I was the parent, but God is the One in control of my little girl's life. He just chooses to work through me to parent her. He was working His master plan. He would go with her. He would see her through the good and the bad. The Lord would direct her steps. I began to understand what familiar passages like Proverbs 16:9 said, "In their hearts humans plan their course, but the Lord establishes their steps" (NIV) or Jeremiah 10:23, "Lord, I know that people's lives are not their own; it is not for them to direct their steps" (NIV).

Regardless of what type school your child attends, all us moms must come to terms with the fact that though we're the parent, God is ultimately The Parent. We must acknowledge it's really up to God to direct their steps.

When your children are in public school, you have limited influence. This is difficult for a Christian parent. We can influence our child and the school through volunteering, helping in the classroom (which I strongly recommend), but the absolute best way and most guaranteed way to influence our children and their school is through prayer. After all, God loves your children more than you do or even can.

Trust God and pray about everything: teachers, principal, children's friends, lunch ladies, cafeteria duty, and Christians in the school to walk with God and direct your child when you can't. I could go on and on, but the thing I find most helpful is just asking God what to pray. Our worry and fear do nothing for our children. Prayer does.

God will help us to let go and trust Him with our children, but we ought to also be spiritual warriors by covering them and their school in prayer.

Tracy

Homeschool. So often I speak to moms who tell me they want to homeschool but feel ill equipped. My response is to tell them that we all homeschool.

From the moment your child is placed in your arms, you are the teacher. Your child learns everything important through the lens you provide. God designed it this way. We are to teach our children. Deuteronomy 11:19 tell us to teach what God says to our children—as a natural part of everyday life—when we are home, out walking, before bed, and when we wake up.

Just a few generations ago, homeschooling was the ONLY option. Today, it is still a great one. Probably one of the biggest hurdles to homeschooling is feeling like you can't do it. As with other things in modern life, we often choose to rely on experts, but we must be careful not to relinquish the charge the Lord has given us for teaching our little ones.

If you are considering homeschool for your children, I want to encourage you on your journey. Many moms are on their knees at the thought of homeschooling, believing everything their child does and becomes is solely their responsibility. It's common for moms to feel that 24-hour-a-day burden for feeding, training, teaching and growing a gaggle of tiny humans.

My response to that is: do not flatter yourself sister, God has got this! You are His instrument, but they are His children, so relax in the Lord and allow His peace to work in you.

It is so easy to allow the convenience of modern medicine to convince us the doctors are experts on our child's health, but Mommas know when something is not right and many a mother has pushed until a doctor has been able to improve the care, diagnosis or treatment of her child. But it begins at home—it begins by knowing the Great Physician and trusting in Him alone.

School is quite similar. There are so many options these days: public or government-funded schools, private schools, religious schools and so on. Then there are homeschools and varying styles of home education: classical, free range or unschooling, traditional, online and so many more. No wonder mothers feel overwhelmed and ill equipped. We have been taught to believe that the teachers are the only experts in education, and we have nothing to do but oversee projects and get them to school on time—that is simply not the case.

Now, do not get me wrong. There are many wonderful educators in each of the settings above, but none of them is the expert on your child. Each child and each season are an opportunity to learn or learn again. So do not fear. YOU CAN DO THIS!

Just like with medicine, the Lord puts people/experts in your path. You choose what is right for your child. You choose the best teacher/school/tutor/book and time to train and teach your child. For different children at different times you may make different choices, and all can be good. I have known families who have students in each of these schools simultaneously. There is no right answer that fits every child.

Sister, if the Lord is calling you to homeschool, He will equip you.

Becoming a homeschool mom is much like becoming a mom—a bit of labor and voila, a baby! Now what?

Now, we pray.

Purposefully do the work the Lord has for you to do.

Remember to do all you do as unto Him.

Affirm that your students are His children.

Yield your desire to be perfect.

Have fun and remember Proverbs 25:2: "It is the glory of God to conceal things, but the glory of kings is to search things out" (ESV). Start simple and start early. Read GOOD books—read out loud and read a bit above their level. Start where you are and just begin. Then before you know it, you are homeschooling!

Angela

Private school. As a teacher and a mom, I have been in all three realms: public school, private school, and homeschool. My sons attended all three types. I have taught all three types. I have learned what works well (and what doesn't work so well) in all three situations. As much as these three options differ, they have one thing in common—prayer is mandatory.

If you are choosing to send your children to private school—especially a private Christian school—you will likely find some wonderful programs and often quite rigorous academics. It can be a nice, comfortable feeling to know your child is being challenged academically and taught everything with a Christian worldview. You might find yourself assuming everything is going swimmingly, eventually not overseeing things the way you would if your child was in a public school or homeschooled. In short—don't! We are still responsible for what our children are learning—biblically, academically, and socially—even if we allow others to teach them at a private Christian school.

We have some wonderful Christian schools in our nation that truly strive to offer the best of it all, but—and most are honest enough to admit it—it's not a perfect world. Therefore, there are no perfect schools. We have been affiliated with some wonderful ones over the years that offer outstanding programs, but that has never diminished the duty God assigned to my husband and me for our children. It is vital for your children to know you are serious about their education—in knowing God and what they learn in school.

As with any school with multiple children in a classroom, a teacher can only do so much. Children do not all learn the same way. Often, there is just one teacher to ten or more students. The greater disparity in that ratio, the less individual attention and the more things occur off a teacher's radar. Children will still need help at some point with their studies; they might have to deal with a bully; there might be peer pressure to resist. Children need their parents to be involved and aware of what goes on—biblically, academically, and socially—just as much in a private school as anywhere else.

So, spiritual warrior women, your children need you and your prayers as they attend private school, public school, or homeschool. Your children's public, private, or homeschool needs you and your prayers, too. Let's be there for them as we follow God's command to teach our children.

Dear God, thank You for my children. Please help me remember they are indeed Yours, and I am blessed to enjoy them as Your good work. Please help me train them up in the way they should go and remember You have a plan for them. Please help me equip them for the calling You have placed on their lives. Please strengthen me each day and forgive me when I fall short. Please help me place them in Your loving care. In Jesus' Name, Amen.

My Prayers for Teaching My Children:

_____

_____

_____

_____

_____

_____

_____

_____

_____

Chapter 29

Pay Attention

with Becky Wangner

❧

"The Lord is near to all who call upon Him, to all who call upon Him in truth." Psalms 145:18

Several years ago, I prayed a very specific prayer. My husband and I adopted four children from orphanages and decided that our "quiver was full." However, our hearts were still broken for the number of orphans still unadopted. One night, I awoke and couldn't go back to sleep. I spent some time praying with one thing on my mind. In my prayer journal I wrote: "God, we are finished adopting children, but I need for You to tell us what we should do next. What is Your will for us?"

After I finished praying, I closed my book and surfed the

internet for college options for my oldest son. Just minutes into the search, a pop-up came on the screen—a promo for a tiny book titled, *Fields of the Fatherless*. I stopped to read the blurb on the cover. Roughly quoting, it read something like this: "Do you want to know the heart of God? In His word, He repeatedly mentions His compassion for three groups of people: The widow, the fatherless, and the sojourner (or stranger). God has already revealed His heart for these three groups—we don't have to wonder if it is His will to help them. We may not be able to adopt, but shouldn't our passions be the same as God's passions?"

This got my attention! I had just prayed a very specific prayer asking God to reveal His will for us now. I pulled out my prayer journal again and wrote the number 10. I asked God to allow my husband and me to help 10 orphans find families. I closed the book and went to bed.

The next morning, an old friend called to catch me up on her new job with an international adoption group. They were looking for host homes for two weeks in the Dallas area for a group of Russian orphans. I paused for a moment, then told her maybe God was leading them to my small town instead of Dallas. She told me they were looking in a more populous area since it was difficult to find host families during the holidays. I convinced her to give our town a try, and she received permission to bring them. I was assigned the task of finding host families for the "Christmas in America" tour. I didn't tell her I was asking God for more than just vacation hosts—I was asking for adoptive families.

I found out she was only bringing 10 children. I have to admit my heart sank a bit when I realized, to hit the number I had prayed for, every single child on this tour would have to be adopted. Of course, I thought if there were 30 kids, it would be much easier to find forever homes for 10 of them—the odds would be much more in our favor.

When the Christmas in America bus pulled up in our small town, it let off ten of the most pitiful, pale, ragged-looking orphans I had ever seen. They were aged 7 to 14 years old—the ages rarely considered by adoptive families.

But God did what only God does. After two amazing weeks with these kids, enough families stepped forward to adopt all 10 of them! It was truly a Christmas miracle like I've never seen before or since. While waiting on the adoption process to be completed—about six months—the children returned to Russia. Once done, the adoptive parents would be allowed to pick up their children.

Sadly, tragedy struck as the last couple traveled to Russia for their son. The night before the court proceeding, the adoptive mother died of an aneurysm. The adoption was canceled since Russia would not allow single fathers to adopt.

My husband flew over to help transport her body home and life became a blur. I wondered: Did I hear God wrong? Wouldn't all 10 kids be coming home? How could such a happy story turn so tragic? The husband was distraught, mourning his wife and now the son he had already grown to love.

But God was still working.

In another miraculous turn of events, the Russian court made an unprecedented exception for him and allowed the adoption. He and his three daughters joyously welcomed their new family member. God saw that all ten children made it home something only He could have orchestrated.

Soon after, I looked up the author of the book displayed in the pop-up on my screen that sleepless night. I wanted to share with him the impact the "computer spam" had on me and all those children. I found his phone number and called him. I shared the whole story: the pop-up ad on the computer, how it led to 10 children finding families, and how other families in our town were now inspired to adopt. When he responded, he sounded puzzled and hesitated. Then he said, "That can't be right."

Are you ready for this?

His book had no presence on the internet. He did not have a pop-up ad, and he wasn't sure how I even came across his book since, at that time, he had not yet distributed or advertised it!

Wow.

I believe God truly delights in answering specific prayers.

God wants us to be acutely attuned to the passions and desires of *His* heart. Psalms 145:18 tells us, "The Lord is near to all who call upon Him, to all who call upon Him in truth." Since the Christmas in America tour miracle, my husband and I began making "kingdom lists"—an ever-changing list of people or causes or promptings God places on our hearts that need attention. In James 1:27 we read, "Religion that is pure and undefiled before God the Father is this: to visit orphans and widows in their affliction, and to keep oneself unstained from the world" (ESV). These lists are how we've come to know some of the most precious people we've ever met—widows, international students, foster care graduates——those people who are helpless in the world's eyes, but never leave the focus of God's eyes.

Spiritual warrior women, God may be speaking to you today—through the Word of God, promptings of the Spirit, His still-small voice, or maybe even spam. Are you paying attention?

Dear God, please help me to always call upon You in truth. Help me be attuned to what You desire. Please help me have ears to hear You and to pay attention to what You are showing me. In Jesus' Name, Amen.

What God Has Placed on My Heart:

_____

_____

_____

_____

_____

_____

_____

_____

Chapter 30

Have a Heart of Hospitality

with Carrie Gill

⟨◦⟩

"Do not neglect to show hospitality to strangers, for thereby some have entertained angels unawares." Hebrews 13:2, ESV

If you look up the definition of hospitality*, this is what you'll find: the friendly and generous reception and entertainment of guests, visitors, or strangers. I am always surprised when people tell me I am hospitable. They say things like, "Every time we come to your house, it is full of people coming, going, eating, studying, laughing, crying..." The reason it surprises me is because I don't "feel" generous, friendly, or much like entertaining. My house is usually in disarray. The laundry is piled high and I am just plain tired and need to rest.

But what I have learned is none of that matters. People don't care. They just need to feel welcomed and wanted.

Most of the devotionals I have read on hospitality focus on the treatment of the guests—and that's great! But I want to turn that all around and explain how I became the one who received the blessing—through having a heart of hospitality.

Let me tell you the story. It began with Carol. She spent years in my house as a school-aged friend of my daughter. She grew from an energetic girl—you know, the one still up at four in the morning during a sleepover—to a lovely young woman. Over the years, our whole family fell in love with her.

As time went on and life unfolded, my granddaughter was born, and she and my daughter lived with us. Life was full, busy, challenging, beautiful, and revolved around my precious granddaughter. I cherished every moment they lived with us, knowing that one day they would move out. I did lots of praying about that. I knew it would be heartbreaking when the time came, although the circumstances that led up to it were the opposite. My daughter fell in love with a wonderful, Christian young man. Before we knew it, they were married and the time had arrived for them to begin their life together—which meant my granddaughter, who had filled every moment of my every day—would be going with them. Please don't misunderstand—I was thrilled with all of it! It was God's blessing on me, my husband, my daughter, and my granddaughter. I just knew the change would be hard. They had lived with us for six and a half years.

I braced for the grieving I expected to fill the void, but it never came. Carol did. She came to our home the very same week under some difficult circumstances of her own and stayed with us for six weeks. We grew to love her even more than before and she became part of our family.

And I was the one who received the blessing. God provided, comforted me, and made the transitions wonderful. When I expected grieving and heartache, I was given joy overflowing and a new definition of hospitality. So now I define hospitality this way: late nights, early mornings, being eaten out of house and home, tears, laughter, smiles, hugs, lots of bedsheets needing changed, unfinished chores, changes of plans, and dirty dishes.

In other words, overflowing blessing.

Hebrews 13:16 tells us, "Do not neglect to do good and to share what you have, for such sacrifices are pleasing to God" (ESV). Notice here it does not say to make sure your house is perfect first or that your lives have to be perfect first. We are simply supposed to have a heart of hospitality.

It's very easy to become caught up in our own lives and what we have going on. Or maybe we worry too much over the condition of our house. It does not take perfect or fancy décor to welcome someone and give an attentive ear. In fact, we don't even have to "feel" perfectly hospitable. 1 Peter 4:9 says to "Show hospitality to one another without grumbling" (ESV). That seems pretty doable, doesn't it?

Having a heart of hospitality is meant to be a natural part of our lives as spiritual warrior women. I am reminded of Matthew 25:34-36, 40: "For I was hungry and you gave me food, I was thirsty and you gave me drink, I was a stranger and you welcomed me, I was naked and you clothed me, I was sick and you visited me, I was in prison and you came to me...'Truly, I say to you, as you did it to one of the least of these my brothers, you did it to Me'" (ESV). A small act can have lifelong impact. Sometimes a kind word is all it takes to change the trajectory of someone's life.

What I have learned most is that a heart of hospitality is a gift. Hebrews 13:2 says, "Do not neglect to show hospitality to strangers, for thereby some have entertained angels unawares" (ESV). In my case, I knew I was entertaining an "angel" named Carol, but I had no idea that I would be the one receiving the blessing.

Dear God, please give me a heart of hospitality. Help me show kindness the way You would have me. Let me not neglect to do good and share what I have. May it be a pleasing sacrifice to You. In Jesus' Name, Amen.

Examples of Hospitality in the Bible:

_____

_____

_____

_____

_____

_____

_____

_____

_____

_____

* https://www.lexico.com/en/definition/hospitality

Going Deeper

Make Camp in the Wilderness

with Caroline George

"Do not be afraid. Stand firm and you will see the deliverance the Lord will bring you today." Exodus 14:13, NIV

We all know the wilderness—those moments without a greener horizon in sight, where we're uncomfortable and desperate. In those desolate places, we question if God will provide a way out. But what if we're not meant to rush the wilderness process? What if God wants to give us abundance in times of fear and doubt, and all we need to do is make camp?

I remember the day God called me—more like shoved me—into the wilderness.

That morning, I received news via text message that the church ministry job I had arranged for after college graduation fell through. No explanation. No further details.

My dreams crumbled, spiraling me into confusion. For years, I'd served at my home church in Nashville. I felt called into ministry and expected to work at the same church after graduation. The abrupt news didn't make sense. Why would God lead me this way if He didn't want me in ministry? Why would He uproot me after years of planting?

One message started a two-year-long wilderness season. I returned to Nashville after months away at an internship to find my home church in shambles, my post-grad plans nonexistent, and relationships ended.

By graduation, my entire life in Nashville had fallen apart.

Next thing I knew, I stood in my parents' basement with a pile of suitcases, not sure what to do next.

Merriam-Webster dictionary defines *wilderness* as a "bewildering situation" and "an empty or pathless region." I'm sure we can agree that whenever God leads us out of our comfort zones and into challenging times, we feel as though we're in uncharted territory. We search for answers—ways out of the trials. We squint our eyes and try to gain a sense of direction.

Each of us responds to the wilderness in different ways. Sometimes we beg God for an escape or end, and we get discouraged when He doesn't immediately answer our prayers.

Other times, we hunker down, trudge forward, and hope we'll survive.

But God designed the wilderness to be more than something we endure. In those uncertain times, He wants to shower us with provision and guidance, but we must choose to stop looking for an escape and instead ask Him to reveal His purpose.

We must make camp in the wilderness.

Into the Wilderness

When Pharaoh let the children of Israel go, God did not lead them on the road through Philistine country, though that was shorter. "For God said, 'If they face war, they might change their minds and return to Egypt.' So God led the people around by the desert road toward the Red Sea" (Exodus 13:17-18, NIV).

God cares about us more than He does our timeline.

God knew what the Israelites had endured, saw their brokenness. The wilderness wasn't a detour but a rescue. It was a place where God would reveal His character to His chosen people and establish an intimate relationship with them.

Like with the Israelites, God sees our injuries. He knows our past, present, and future—and what must happen within our hearts before we're ready to enter the "Promised Land." Of course, the Promised Land will look different for each of us. Maybe it's a season of peace, a divine calling, or a career that seems impossible.

When I moved back to my family home, I was discouraged.

During one of many prayer walks, I asked God *why*. Why did He bring me home and let my life in Nashville fall apart? At that moment, I felt from the Lord: "I brought you into the wilderness to fulfill my plans for you."

Since I was a child, my dream had been to write full time. I had self-published two books in high school and a third book with a traditional publisher while in college. An author career seemed unrealistic, though. I needed to think about money, adulthood, family expectations, and the call to ministry.

For two years, I wrote book after book. My agent sent the manuscripts to acquisitions editors, and I waited. I checked my inbox. I prayed and hoped—and cried a lot. The wait dragged on. People questioned my resolve; I doubted God's direction. I wanted safety and surety, not the fear of what might happen if God didn't come through. He was taking *too long*. Didn't He see my desperation?

One Sunday morning, part of the message at church was: "It was one thing for God to take the Israelites out of Egypt. It was a whole other thing for God to take Egypt out of the Israelites." That's when I realized my wilderness wasn't about book deals and success. God wanted to take "Egypt" out of me. He wanted to heal me from past hurt and fulfill His will for me.

God functions on a big-picture timeline. Our wilderness seasons will end. Breakthrough will come. But we can't overlook the true purpose of the wilderness—to grow closer to the Lord as He fulfills His will in our lives.

God had a plan for the Israelites' desert season. He has a plan for ours, too.

God's Wilderness Battle Plan

The wilderness seems full of confusion, but in the uncertainty, we have a certain God who guides us forward and always provides for our needs.

Exodus 13-14 proves God never leaves us. The times we can't see Him in front of us likely means He's behind, protecting us from unseen forces: "Then the angel of God, who had been traveling in front of Israel's army, withdrew and went behind them. The pillar of cloud also moved from in front and stood behind them, coming between the armies of Egypt and Israel. Throughout the night the cloud brought darkness to one side and light to the other side; so neither went near the other all night long (Exodus 14:19-20, NIV).

God goes before us and behind us. He's a protective God. He also strategizes with His kingdom in mind.

During my two-year-long wilderness season, people said to me, "Why do you stay here when you could alter your situation?" Each time, I responded with, "I want Plan A."

Yes, God redeems our mistakes and works all things for His glory and our good. He puts us back on track when we go astray. But I didn't want to settle for Plan B or C—what might happen if I went my own way and let God redeem later. I wanted His best plan.

My circumstance seemed like a setback. I didn't have a job or a plan. Regardless, I clung to the belief that God's will would somehow be done.

When the Israelites saw Pharaoh's army approaching, they panicked and longed for Egypt—a place of captivity—because it seemed familiar and safe.

Moses answered the people, "Do not be afraid. Stand firm and you will see the deliverance the Lord will bring you today. The Egyptians you see today you will never see again. The Lord will fight for you; you need only to be still" (Exodus 14:13-14, NIV).

Aren't we like the Israelites? We venture into the wilderness, gung-ho to reach the "Promised Land." Then, an enemy appears. Our hope dwindles. And we crave a *not-so-great* past rather than face the uncertainty—and dependency—of pursuing God's will for our lives.

God will deliver us and fight on our behalf. If He guides us in, He will make a way out. *God receives the glory.*

In Exodus 14:4, God says, "But I will gain glory for myself through Pharaoh and all his army, and the Egyptians will know that I am Lord" (NIV).

God wanted to show them He wasn't a god but *the* God.

God's wilderness battle plans involve tactics that show His power and faithfulness. Not only do wilderness seasons give us personal testimonies that can bring God glory, they display *who He is* to others. We're but a small part of the miraculous story God wants to tell through us when we are willing.

Out of the Wilderness

Then the Lord said to Moses, "Why are you crying out to Me? Tell the Israelites to move on. Raise your staff and stretch out your hand over the sea to divide the water so that the Israelites can go through the sea on dry ground" (Exodus 14:15-16, NIV).

Moses had to respond to God's instructions and step out in faith. As he raised his staff, he must've realized he would look foolish if God didn't part the waters. Of course, believing God isn't always the safe or practical choice.

On top of making a physical declaration of obedience and faith, Moses told the Israelites to move forward before the waters even parted.

There are times when God calls us to take a step of faith out of obedience and then trust Him to work out His perfect plan. We might have doubts. (Even Jesus' disciples had doubts at times.)

When we obey God, He parts the waters.

"Then Moses stretched out his hand over the sea, and all that night the Lord drove the sea back with a strong east wind and turned it into dry land. The waters were divided, and the Israelites went through the sea on dry ground, with a wall of water on their right and on their left. (Exodus 14:21-22, NIV).

The Promised Land

God did a miracle in my life. Two years after I stepped into the wilderness, my dream publisher offered a three-book contract, which surpassed all expectations. By that point, I was no longer praying for success, rather that God would finish what He started.

As I gathered with friends and family to sign the contract, I realized my wilderness season wasn't just for me. So many people had witnessed the process.

When God parted the "sea" in my life, He showed His faithfulness to others.

The wilderness wasn't a setback. It put me on the right course. Now I have a personal testimony of God's provision. My story is His victory.

Making camp in the wilderness means to slow down and rely on the Father. It means to step out in faith and wait for God to do a miracle. Yes, He will guide us through the wilderness.

Chapter 31

Show Grace Under Pressure

with Heather Stoner

"She is clothed in strength and dignity and she laughs without fear of the future. When she speaks, her words are wise and she gives instructions with kindness." Proverbs 31:25-26

What do you think of when you hear the word, "grace?" Do you think of your mother, an aunt, or maybe an older lady from church? When I was a little girl, I remember getting to go to a grown up's luncheon at the local country club. For a farm girl this was unfamiliar territory and quite a huge deal! I was seated across from a beautiful woman. I watched her closely and was mesmerized by how she could dab her mouth with her white, linen napkin and not get red lipstick on it. To my ten-year-old self, she was the epitome of grace. Perhaps when you hear the word, "grace," glamorous and famous women like Grace Kelly or Kate Middleton come to mind. You know, the type who are always saying the perfect compliment or witty comment at the proper time; always doing the right thing in public—and looking perfect while doing it, I might add!

For me, in my own hectic daily life, I often put the word, "grace," into the phrase, "grace under fire." That is what I am called to every moment of every day in my line of work in the political arena. My corner of the political arena involves organizing events for political figures. Some are small and some are huge. The large (and small) events take months of planning and coordinating. There are security considerations, schedules, changes, moods, personalities, time crunches, budgets, attendees, catering, tickets, advertising, and more. But the really tough part of the job is that it requires the utmost composure at all times—no matter how many times and how many things go wrong and not as planned! Someone recently told me that I am like a swan on top of the water but like a duck underneath paddling like mad. I have to say, that is pretty accurate. It probably describes most of us as we "manage" our day-to-day lives. We need grace to get through the day. Some days, of course, it feels like we need it more than others, but in reality, we need God's grace every moment of every day, whether or not the day is going along according to our plans.

And isn't it wonderful that God gives us His grace every day? In 2 Corinthians 12:9 it says, "My grace is sufficient for you, for My strength is made perfect in weakness." This is such a great reminder as we juggle a zillion things at a time every day. The secret to maintaining grace under pressure is that we can't do it! It is God's grace that makes it possible.

2 Timothy 1:9 tells us God "called us to a holy calling, not because of our works but because of His own purpose and grace, which He gave us in Christ Jesus before the ages began." Because God has shown us so much grace in Jesus for the forgiveness of sins, and because He gives us grace to live day by day, we can extend grace to others.

I am often giving instructions to volunteers and interns during the preparation for a big event. It involves so many moving parts that it is quite stressful for everyone. Proverbs 31:25-26 must stay at the forefront of my mind—giving instructions with kindness, representing a Christ-like attitude in the heat of the moment and often with very little sleep.

Grace takes courage! It takes grace and courage to make a beautiful meal for family members who have not been caring or are critical. It takes grace to show kindness to others who are not the same way in return. It takes grace and courage to stand on your convictions and face opposition. It takes grace and courage to live out your life in a way that draws those around you to Christ; to leave a sweet fragrance that goes with the mention of your name and points those who think of you to the One who gives you peace in the midst of the storm.

Spiritual warrior women, I believe we can walk out our days with grace and giving grace because God has shown us such grace in His forgiveness. Thankfully, as Lamentations 3:23 says,

His mercies are new every morning, which is good because I usually use mine up before 3 P.M.! And because "His mercies never come to an end" (Lamentations 3:22), we, too, can be clothed in strength and dignity, not fear the future, and show grace under pressure.

Dear God, each day has its own new challenges. Today, I lay down my own emotions and reactions. Please help me walk out each encounter, activity and daily task with GRACE. May my words be wise, and my instructions be given with kindness. I pray that I will react with a graciousness that can only come from You and reflects your love and kindness for those around me. In Jesus' Name, Amen.

How God Shows Grace to Me and How I Can Show Grace to Others:

_____

_____

_____

_____

_____

_____

_____

_____

_____

Chapter 32

Enter the Fray

with Bunni Pounds

"As You sent Me into the world, I also have sent them into the world." John 17:15-18

Have you **entered the fray**—answered God's call and stepped out on the water to do something you have never done before?

I ran for Congress. It was the hardest thing I have ever done. It was brutal, exhausting, and full of incredible pressure I wouldn't wish on anyone—but it also was extremely rewarding. I like to say to others: You haven't lived 'til you have had almost $1,000,000 in negative advertising against you and your family. It's a whole new level.

Let me just preface this by saying: I am not a Muslim that converted to Jesus and had to leave my family over the fear of being killed. I don't understand the slaughter of Coptic Christians in Egypt and what they endure. My father died from a brain tumor, but he didn't suffer, so I have never had to watch a loved one endure sickness and die in pain. But from an American point of view, after running for Congress, I have a little deeper understanding of suffering.

When I was an eighteen-year-old Bible school student, I said "Yes" to God's leadership in my life forever. The Scripture on my heart was Philippians 1:29: "For to you it has been granted on behalf of Christ, not only to believe in Him, but also to suffer for His sake."

I thought I would be moving to Rwanda to help children who were starving. I thought I was going to end up a martyr in North Africa or a caretaker of orphans in Latin America. I told God I would leave all the comforts of my American lifestyle and go plant churches wherever He led me—even to the ends of the earth.

None of those scenarios happened.

What did happen was that my best friend, Tim Pounds, proposed marriage at a pancake restaurant (you can't make this stuff up), and I ended up staying in America, having babies and running small businesses we started.

Ten years later, I had a career as a full-time political consultant, working with members of Congress, state senators and county officials. I had said "Yes" to Jesus as He led me in another assignment. I did my best to live out my calling faithfully day by day, as a missionary to America—walking beside the leaders of our nation. I could speak hope to them, take them to the wisdom found in the Word of God, and impact the nation in small ways through the relationships I had with leaders of our country.

Then the main member of Congress for whom I had worked for over 10 years announced his retirement. I couldn't find his replacement—everyone said no. It became apparent I was the one with a burden from the Lord for the district. I even knew the political people throughout the area. I knew federal public policy, I knew business, and I was ready for an adventure. Was I ready for this—really?

After a weekend of prayer and fasting, I felt the call of God. I said "Yes." I was about to truly **enter the fray**.

Approximately one month later, I was running for Congress.

I campaigned hard from December 2017 to May 2018. In less than five months, a woman unknown to 40,000 primary voters had to become the person they should elect. We had an amazing team—consultants, associates, volunteers, and key people who endorsed me all over the state. It appeared we were in a place like Esther 4:14, "for such a time as this."

With almost a million dollars raised in less than five months, I was the only woman in 2018 on the Republican Congressional races in Texas out of 46 candidates that made it to the runoff ballot. I was the only person in the

U.S. during the 2018 primary season endorsed by Vice President Mike Pence (that is a whole miracle story on its own for another book).

All this while, a super PAC spent almost $500,000 against me calling me a "swamp creature" and a "Washington insider" because I worked for members of Congress, including the incumbent, for 10 years. But God was there giving me courage, boldness, and favor in the midst of it. His presence in this hard season was the most tangible in my life, and I was living my purpose.

John 17 is one of the most important chapters in the Bible to me. It is the High Priestly prayer of Jesus—one of His final prayers before He went to the cross and suffered for us.

In John 17 we read, even in His final hours on this earth, Jesus' heart yearning for us to know Him, to be one in Him, and to be protected from the evil one. "I do not pray that You should take them out of the world, but that You should keep them from the evil one." John 17:15

God doesn't want us to disengage from the world and from our culture. He wants us to engage! He doesn't want us to stop in fear on the sidelines of the battle, He wants us to enter the fray knowing He is with us in the battle. Don't be afraid! The battle is where the sweetness is found and where Jesus is so near and dear.

Jesus never promised we wouldn't experience hard times, pain, or suffering as Christians, but He did promise that He would walk with us through them, and in John 17, He is praying to KEEP us from the evil one.

It brings me so much comfort that Jesus is standing at the right hand of the Father, always praying for you and me. He is the GREAT Intercessor. He doesn't slumber or sleep.

"Therefore He is also able to save to the uttermost those who come to God through Him, since He always lives to make intercession for them" (Hebrews 7:25).

With Jesus with me—how can I not live my life to the fullest? How can I cower back and not be on the front lines of my life?

Spiritual warrior women, it is time we live the fullest adventure of our lives. It is time that we yield to His voice in obedience. Perhaps we will inspire others to also enter the fray.

Dear God, I say "Yes" again today. I will believe in You and Your purposes for my life and follow where You lead. In Jesus' Name, Amen.

How I am Preparing to Enter the Fray Where God Leads Me:

_____

_____

_____

_____

_____

_____

_____

194

Chapter 33

Pray for Your Nation

with Sheryl Coffey

❦

"Blessed is the nation whose God is the Lord." Psalms 33:12

4:26 p.m. I will always remember that time of day. It was the time I heard a sweet call from my little son, Jonathan. He wanted to pray with me most every afternoon. Although my dear boy died just before turning two years old—more than forty years ago—his voice still sweetly rings in my ears, and the call to pray sounds loudly in my heart.

And so, I pray. Every day. I set my phone alarm for 4:26 as my reminder to pause and lift up important matters to our Heavenly Father. I pray for our nation on a daily basis, placing the President, the Vice-President, and other elected officials in God's hands. Not only is it something I do as a special remembrance of my son, but it is something I do out of obedience to God.

The Bible tells us in Psalms 33:12, "Blessed is the nation whose God is the Lord." I don't know about you, but that is the type of nation I desire to live in—the kind that honors God and acknowledges that it is His protection and guidance we need. I want to live in a nation that is unafraid and unashamed to recognize its Christian heritage and be a "shining city on a hill" (Matthew 5:14). But this does not happen on its own, nor does it remain on its own.

The beautiful freedoms we take for granted were paid for with blood, sweat, tears, and precious lives. There is a still a war raging against those freedoms, but it is more of a spiritual war, than one we see with our eyes. This is why it is absolutely necessary that we make and take time to pray for the country in which we live.

But we should not stop there. Our state and local governments, school boards, etc., need to be brought before the Lord. After all, they make decisions that affect all of us. Let us do what God has commanded us to do in 1 Timothy 2:1-2: "Therefore I exhort first of all that supplications, prayers, intercessions, and giving of thanks be made for all men, for kings and all who are in authority, that we may lead a quiet and peaceable life in all godliness and reverence."

But there's more to this passage. Verses three and four explain, "For this is good and acceptable in the sight of God our Savior, who desires all men to be saved and to come to the knowledge of the truth." We must pray for our nation not only for our own lives but to preserve our God-ordained freedoms, so that we may freely live and share the Gospel.

Of course, God's Word will go forth, regardless of what the circumstances are—but let us take care to work "while it is day; [for] the night is coming when no one can work" (John 9:4).

Another person I regularly lift up in prayer is the First Lady. She is another person who influences a great many others, including the President. But she is also a wife and mother as many of us are, with the added pressures of living under public scrutiny. I pray for her according to II Kings 4:26. In this passage, a Shunamite woman, who had no children of her own, showed great care for Elisha the prophet. Elisha told her she would have a son, and a year later, she did. However, the child grew ill and died. The woman tracked Elisha down in her distress. His words to her were, "Is it well with you? Is it well with your husband? Is it well with your son?" Elisha brought the son back to life and all was well.

I pray for the First Lady that all is well with her. This brings me back to why we must pray for our nation. We want it to be well with us, with our husbands, and with our children. The responsibility is on the shoulders of God's children, especially when there is trouble in the land and the nation has gone astray from the path of righteousness. We, as God's people, are instructed in II Chronicles 7:14, "If My people who are called by My name will humble themselves, and pray and seek My face, and turn from their wicked ways, then I will hear them from heaven, and will forgive their sin and heal their land."

Spiritual warrior women, let it begin with us and in our homes. Let us pray for our families, our neighborhoods, cities, states, and our nation. Jeremiah 29:7 tells us to pray for the peace of the city where He has us, "for in its peace [we] will have peace."

Let us lift up all those God has placed in government, so it may be well with us and we may live in peace and freedom to share the Gospel. Take a moment each day, at 4:26 or at another time, to pray for our nation so we may have the blessing to live in a nation "whose God is the Lord" (Psalms 33:12).

Dear God, thank You for giving us this beautiful country. I lift it to You and ask for Your guidance, protection, and blessing. Forgive us as a nation for going astray. Help us turn back to You. In Jesus' Name, Amen.

Prayers for Our Nation, My State, City, Neighborhood, Family, and Those in Government:

_____

_____

_____

_____

_____

_____

Chapter 34

Rescue the Lost

with Nicole Fitzpatrick

"No weapon formed against you shall prosper." Isaiah 54:17

My husband, Jason, and I have been married for over 27 years. We live and work in Mexico among the poor and marginalized descendants of Aztec Indians, sharing the Gospel with many for the first time. For 29 years, Jason and I have planted churches, started drug rehabs, and since 2004, we have rescued lost children.

At our Village Children's Home, we take in abandoned, abused, and orphaned children, who were at risk or homeless. Many of these precious little ones come out of sex trafficking. We rescue them. Then I do my best to find some of them a family or

199

foster family. Others are here for just a few short months during a court case until they are placed with a permanent family. And some remain with us. But to all of them, we become Mama and Papa—a forever family. Kids that I rescued 15 years ago still call me, come over, and we are still Mama and Papa.

Most people believe trafficking occurs as seen on popular shows such as "Taken" (and that does happen), but the reality is nearly ninety percent of minors are rented and sold by the ones who should be caring for and protecting them—primarily a stepdad, or mom's boyfriend. Traffickers prey upon young single moms (or young widows) who live in poverty. They begin dating her and convincing her of their love. Many times, the trafficking begins with her. Once they are under his rule and their conscious is seared, they move in on the little girls.

Sometimes the victims are orphans, so their grandparents or aunt or uncle rents them to put their own kids through school or simply to put food on the table to feed them all. Some of my cases were abandoned kids on the streets and their older brothers began renting them to men at ages four and five—for survival. It puts food in their stomachs.

Some of the children we have rescued were simply permanently sold by their impoverished, widowed, or abandoned mother to traffickers who travel and offer them as "fresh meat." And some of my kids are second or third generation brothel babies, and I rescue them from the brothel bars.

Each rescue is so very distinct, yet so similarly sad.

Many of those we rescue are boys, but the majority are girls. Sometimes, I see small children in public, recognize the signs, investigate, and move in. Other times, I receive an anonymous phone call, from someone who knows what I do, or someone I helped in the past. They hear of another victim, and they inform me of a small child they suspect is being sold or rented, etc. Sometimes I negotiate with the perpetrators to get the child or children. Other times, I partner with state authorities and police to help me. Still other times, I send some of my own team, dressed as state nurses or census agents. They obtain information and take discreet pictures for evidence, and we move in. Then there are times when I just have to move in immediately and worry about legalities later.

Despite what the news says, human trafficking and the child sex trade are only getting worse with growing populations and lawlessness.

The situation is such that virtually all of law enforcement's rights have been taken away and they cannot adequately do their jobs. Just recently, I responded to a night call of a four-year-old raped on a Sunday night. I spoke with that district's mayor. He sent me a patrol truck full of officers, and we moved in. But the armed men had to stand on the dirt road outside of the brothel area and I entered alone—they just stand ready in case I yell, or they hear a shot or a struggle —or if I do not come out. I receive constant threats, have had guns drawn on me—even put to my head once—but God is so faithful and always has the last word. Isaiah 54:17 declares, "No weapon formed against you shall prosper."

It is my heart's call to rescue, restore, and raise children who have suffered this abuse and trafficking. We pray a lot. Each morning, I wake up my 46 children (we always have 35-60 under our roof) and we go downstairs to worship, pray, and read the Bible together.

I understand—albeit in a different form—I know what it means to be lost and in need of rescue.

I met Jason when I was 14 years old and we married four years later. I fell in love with my husband twice. The first time was before we were married. The second time was one year later when, while traveling through Texas, I was thrown through a windshield and landed over 80 feet from my crashed vehicle. I had numerous life-threatening injuries. My heart had to be restarted five times. I came out of a ten-day coma with no memory of who I was or who my husband was. He was a perfect stranger to me. But he went to work to win my heart a second time...and succeeded. We are no strangers to overcoming enormous obstacles. After the accident, I was told I would never bear children, but by the grace of God, I eventually delivered two healthy and beautiful children. But again, God is faithful and always has the last word.

What I have I learned—and am still learning—in doing this is that God is God. Always will be (Malachi 3:6). And He created us as free moral agents, so He will only go as far as we allow Him, because we are His vessels. We choose each day Whom we will serve (Joshua 24:15).

Prayer is first and so very, very essential. But we also have to Go. Sacrifice. Give. Trust. Believe. Risk. Be His ambassadors.

God wakes me at night to pray through things. We anoint the doors and entrances to the Village often and plead the blood of Jesus over each and every person that comes. No matter the addiction, affliction, disease, pain, suffering, brokenness, or abuse, the Gospel has proven to be the cure. Jesus remains our great Healer and Provider.

Dear God, You are God and You always have the last word. Please help me to yield my life fully to Your will. I choose this day to serve You. I want to be Your ambassador. In Jesus' Name, Amen.

Prayers for Those I Know Suffering from Addiction, Affliction, Brokenness, and Abuse:

_____

_____

_____

_____

_____

_____

_____

_____

Chapter 35

Heal from Trauma

with Dr. Grace English

❦

"He heals the brokenhearted and binds up their wounds."
Psalms 147:3

Why is healing from trauma so necessary? Living in the world, you will have trauma of some sort. The trauma could be inflicted by others, or it could be from poor choices you have made in your past. Either way, the Lord doesn't want you to live in that trauma, but instead has come to give you complete healing and freedom from it.

True healing is only found through the power of the Holy Spirit. It is only possible through the blood of Christ that cleanses us from our sins and empowers us to forgive those who have wronged us. So first and foremost, having a personal relationship with Jesus Christ is essential, so He can come into your life and begin the healing work in whatever devastation left behind from past traumas.

I chose to have an abortion at the age of 18. I thought my decision to end my pregnancy would help me out of my crisis, because it was inconvenient for me to have a baby at that time. I believed the lie that abortion was my decision to make, and that it wouldn't hurt me or anyone else.

Shortly after the abortion, I developed bulimia, and started to use drugs and alcohol to numb the pain of the abortion. It would be years later before I realized the decision to end my unborn baby's life had taken a huge emotional and spiritual toll on mine. My life was a mess. My heart had been shattered to pieces, and I finally realized I needed hope and healing from my abortion. I was suffering from Post-Traumatic Stress Disorder (PTSD). Many women and men who have experienced and suffered the loss of their babies through abortion experience PTSD.

The PTSD symptoms I struggled with were guilt, anger, unforgiveness, shame, secrecy, an eating disorder, and unworthiness. This definitely impacted who I was, my relationship with the Lord, and how I related to those closest to me—specifically my husband and my living children. My husband and children deserved more from me.

I found hope and healing through an abortion recovery Bible study class. There, the wounds and anger left behind from the abortion were finally dealt with. I was able to process more of the experience and understand how that abortion had impacted my life. The Lord showed His love and mercy to me and began the healing work in my life —in those raw and deep crevices of my heart and mind—from the trauma that occurred as a result of ending my unborn baby's life.

Spiritual warrior women, my trauma was my abortion, but your trauma could be something else. It could be sexual abuse, abandonment, physical abuse, divorce, death of a loved one, etc. Whatever it is that has shattered your heart, the Lord Jesus wants to come and heal your broken heart. He understands our pain and suffering—those we cause ourselves and those inflicted on us by others.

Psalm 56:8 says, "You have kept count of my tossings; put my tears in Your bottle. Are they not in Your book?" (ESV). Precious daughter, nothing escapes His notice. He knows what you have been through. "When the righteous cry for help, the Lord hears and delivers them out of all their troubles. The Lord is near to the brokenhearted and saves the crushed in spirit" (Psalm 34:17-18, ESV). Whatever your trauma is, know that nothing is too difficult for Him to heal!

Spiritual warrior women, we need the freedom that comes with being healed from trauma. Carrying the weight of it can cause trouble for us and those we love. Jesus does not want us to carry that baggage and suffer even more from it. He made it clear in Matthew 11:28: "Come to me, all who labor and are heavy laden, and I will give you rest" (ESV). Whatever trauma you have experienced, trust your loving Savior to heal you. He came that we may have life and have it more abundantly (John 10:10). He wants to set us free and heal all of our wounds.

Much of Jesus' ministry here on earth involved healing the sick, the afflicted, and "all who were oppressed by the devil" (Acts 10:38, ESV). And Jesus did more than that. He came, lived a sinless life, suffered, died, and rose again so that we might have forgiveness of sins through Him. That is where healing from trauma begins. That is where we gain the ability to forgive those who have wronged us. And that is where we gain "the peace which surpasses all understanding" (Philippians 4:7, ESV). It is to Jesus we go because "He heals the brokenhearted and binds up their wounds" (Psalms 147:3). Trust Him and He will do it!

Dear God, You know the trauma I have experienced in my life. You know what I have caused myself and what others have done. I come to You now and ask You to heal me of all of it. I cast my cares upon You and lay these burdens at Your feet. Please heal me and set me free. Help me forgive where I need to forgive. In Jesus' Name, Amen.

Areas in My Life Where Jesus Has Set Me Free:

_____

_____

_____

_____

_____

_____

Going Deeper

Worship

with Rita Halter Thomas and Dr. Angela Ruark

"...but the hour is coming, and is now here, when the true worshipers will worship the Father in spirit and truth, for the Father is seeking such people to worship Him." John 4:23

Because we've recognized Jesus as our Lord and Savior and the Holy Spirit resides within us, we have been given an arsenal of spiritual weapons. We have everything we need to be spiritual warrior women who are *in* the world but not *of* it. Yet, on this side of heaven, our spiritual growth remains unfinished—there is so much more in store for us.

We are meant to daily grow in our faith and draw near to God. This growth comes from our time spent with Him in prayer, the study of His Word, leaning on Him as we face daily challenges, and more. Worship of God is also an essential part of our spiritual growth. True worship draws us closer to Him. It is an act of obedience. Isaiah 12:5 tells us, "Sing praises to the Lord, for He has done gloriously; let this be made known in all the earth" (ESV).

When someone mentions worship, what comes to mind? You might imagine believers, arms lifted, eyes closed, singing to God. Maybe you are alone at home or in your car. Psalms 96:1 tells us, "Oh, sing to the Lord a new song!" Singing praise songs to God helps us take our eyes off of ourselves and keep them on the Lord and His goodness. There are so many things for which we can praise and worship God: the magnificence of creation, the gift of salvation, the giggles of our children, the beauty that awaits us in Heaven, just to name a few.

While music and singing are wonderful ways to worship God that we should do daily, there is still more: Our very lives can worship God.

What Worship Is

Romans 12:2 provides a description of worship: "present your bodies as a living sacrifice, holy and acceptable to God, which is your spiritual worship" (ESV). Everything we do and say (and think and feel) ought to bring glory to God. As living sacrifices, we must "Put to death what is earthly in [us]..." (Colossians 3:5, ESV) and "take every thought captive to obey Christ" (II Corinthians 10:5, ESV). This is a daily surrender; a continual laying down of our lives at Jesus' feet. Hebrews 12:5 tells us to "continually offer the sacrifice of praise to God, that is, the fruit of our lips, giving thanks to His name." Worship should be a natural result of our walk with Jesus.

As we grow and mature in that walk, we will naturally worship Him more. Especially when we desire a relationship with God that has depth. The opportunity is before us—we can have the closeness with God we read about in Scripture: the kind of faith that worships God no matter what and gives Him all the glory—in times of joy and in the darkest moments of life—even unto death. It's up to us.

Worship comes from a realization that God loved us first while we were unlovable, sacrificed His precious Son on the cross to pay for our sins, then gave the Holy Spirit to those who accept Him as Lord and Savior (1 John 4:19; Romans 3:23-26; Acts, 2:38).

The more we know and understand God, the more we recognize His might, power, and holiness, and the more in awe

211

of Him we become. Psalms 96:9 tells us, "Worship the Lord in the splendor of holiness; tremble before Him all the earth!"

As we worship the Lord, our faith is strengthened. When we recognize God's hand in our circumstance—the good and the bad—our faith grows, and we are able to worship God regardless of our situations. We praise Him through every trial and triumph, and it becomes a powerful testimony.

Worship is also a mighty weapon—one feared by the enemy. It is a weapon that defeats the fiery darts thrown at us; it is a weapon that draws others to the Lord as they see Him work in our lives; and it is a weapon to keep our heads up and our hearts singing.

God is looking for those to enlist in His army. John 4:23 tells us, "but the hour is coming, and is now here, when the true worshipers will worship the Father in spirit and truth, for the Father is seeking such people to worship Him." Are you one of those people?

How We Worship

Worship is reflected in both action and attitude. It might mean attending services faithfully, engaging in fellowship with other believers, serving, giving, studying, praying, fasting, and loving others. Worship is an act of obedience that must be true within our hearts as well. John 4:24 tells us those who worship God "must worship Him in spirit and in truth." We must know the truth—meaning we must always ensure that what we believe and share with others always aligns with what the Bible says.

True worship is anchored in humility and surrendered obedience. It deepens our relationship with the Lord and brings God glory. The humbled, surrendered heart of a believer draws closer to the Lord and produces fruit that draws others to Him, too.

Several years ago, a precious friend survived a car accident that claimed the life of her husband and two children. Prior to this tragedy, it was easy to see the Lord reflected in her life. But afterward, and all these years since, it is even more apparent that the Lord is working in her and through her. She has gained more wisdom, more hope, more love, and more peace. She continues to worship God through it all and is a wonderful example to those around her. Such depth grew from a steadfast worship of the Lord through incredible loss and heartbreak.

Let's face it. It's easy to worship the Lord when everything in our lives seems perfect. At some point, however, we will be affected by some type of heart ache, directly or indirectly.

We must worship God in times of joy, sorrow, and everything in between. A heart of worship recognizes God's sovereign reign over our lives and surrendering to Him *is* worship. Through brokenness, heartbreak, and a sense of helplessness, a heart of worship recognizes hope in the Lord, seeks the Lord, and finds comfort in His presence. A heart of worship runs toward God, not away from Him—even through grief and tragedy. It is a choice we have to make. 1 Chronicles 16:34 tells us, "Oh, give thanks to the Lord, for He is good!"

Worthy of Worship

God is good and He alone is worthy of worship. Revelation 4:11 declares, "You are worthy, O Lord, to receive glory and honor and power; for You created all things, and by Your will they exist and were created." Because God is our Creator, He deserves all our praise.

Exodus 20:3 says, "You shall have no other gods before Me." We find it repeated in Deuteronomy 5:7 and Matthew 4:10. There are no exceptions—not our families, careers, money, or anything else. God comes first.

In Genesis 22, Abraham took Isaac up the mountain to worship the Lord. He revered Him above all including his son—the one God promised to him—and Abraham prepared to sacrifice him.

It's hard to imagine.

Abraham withheld nothing from God. In verses 12 and 13 we read how He provided a ram for the sacrifice. But not just that. God rewarded Abraham by promising to multiply his "descendants as the stars of the heaven" (verse 17) and through them "all the nations of the earth shall be blessed" (verse 18).

Spiritual warrior women, we must ask ourselves—are we holding back? Do we desire God above everything? As followers of Jesus, we honor, serve, and obey Him first and foremost. Jesus says in Matthew 10:37-39, "He who loves father or mother more than Me is not worthy of Me. And he who does not take his cross and follow after Me is not worthy of Me. He who finds his life will lose it, and he who loses his life for My sake will find it."

A life lived in obedience to the Lord, trusting Him, honoring Him, praising Him in all things—that is worship.

Chapter 36

Face a Devastating Diagnosis with Faith

with Linda Dill and Susan Ellsworth

❧

"I will never leave you nor forsake you." Hebrews 13:5

Linda (Mother)

I'll never forget when I received THE CALL. The one you never want. I happened to be at the hospital already for a friend's surgery when I received the diagnosis. Breast cancer. Chemo. Radiation. You only hear bits and pieces. Then shock and tears. But then, resolve. You decide to fight. I prayed and read the Bible. I shaved my hair ahead of time, so I didn't have to lose it.

217

I was extremely ill from the treatments. It was miserable; it was all I could do to survive. And I did survive. After a year or so, the cancer was gone. It has stayed gone for nearly 12 years—at least that particular cancer.

Susan (Daughter)

I felt something in my breast. As an oncology nurse, I had enough background and experience to know it wasn't right. The symptoms I felt were classic, but for three months, the doctors told me I was fine. Even my mammograms showed no signs. But the lump was there and was not going away. So, I insisted on an ultrasound, which led to a biopsy, which led to a double mastectomy and reconstructive surgery.

Linda

Watching your daughter experience breast cancer and all it entails is far worse than experiencing it yourself. She had multiple surgeries. Since she was a cancer nurse, she knew all the worst-case possible outcomes and because of that, so did I.

Let me just say, it was awful. There was a time I was so overwhelmed, I could barely pray. But I did. I prayed for the Lord to be with her and touch her. There was little comfort I could give, but God could and did.

I watched my daughter handle this battle like a true warrior.

Susan

The months between the surgeries and appointments were stressful. All you can do is wait. And pray.

I am the type of person that likes to have things under control. But with this, all my control was gone. Of course, I could choose doctors and other minor things, but with the biggest thing—the life or death thing— there was absolutely nothing I could do.

Well, except give it all to God and trust Him.

It didn't come easy at first. I was mad that I had cancer. And it was inconvenient for everyone—especially me! But by God's grace, I began to look at things in a practical sort of way. This helped tremendously. They mentioned radiation treatment. Ok, fine. I had seen my mom go through it and I had seen plenty of patients go through it. I knew what to expect.

I realized I could live with fear and anxiety or not. I could take it day by day or sit in a corner. I could choose to live a full life now or worry about what-ifs.

I chose to be grateful. Grateful that I was alive and had lived. Of course, I didn't want to die yet and leave my husband, my children, or not see my future grandchildren, but I couldn't dwell on that. I could dwell on enjoying them now and not be afraid of what is going to ultimately happen anyway—to everyone. I chose to face the worst with faith, as it says in Habakkuk 3:17-19, "Though the fig tree may not blossom, nor fruit be on the vines; Though the labor of the olive may fail, and the fields yield no food; Though the flock may be cut off from the fold, and there be no herd in the stalls—Yet I will rejoice in the Lord, I will joy in the God of my salvation. The Lord God is my strength; He will make my feet like deer's feet, and He will make me walk on my high hills."

Linda

There's a saying that attitude determines your altitude. For me, this held true in a biblical sense the second time I had cancer—lung cancer. By the time they found it, my daughter's own cancer treatment was nearly completed. However, my new cancer was stage IV, and they figured I had only a few months to live. But no one told me that! At least if they did, God kept me from hearing it.

This round of cancer was totally different from the other. It began with me not being able to sleep at night. So, I stayed up. I prayed, read the Bible, watched Christian TV shows, did Bible studies, and wrote scriptures in a journal.

And this time, I really grew in the Lord. I had more peace with a far worse diagnosis. Truly, it was the peace that surpasses all understanding from Philippians 4:7. I knew that even if things got really bad, it was ok, because I was right with the Lord. He was with me the whole time. Hebrews 13:5 says, "I will never leave you nor forsake you." I found this to be completely true. God never left me. I prayed Bible verses on healing. I did not know the gravity of my diagnosis, but I knew that cancer could mean death, and God gave me peace through it all.

Then, He healed me.

Mother and Daughter

We don't live here on earth forever, so you need to know where you are going when your time comes. For both of us, it made all the difference to know that if we died, we would go to Heaven. As much as we want to be with our family here as long as we possibly can, Heaven will be so much more wonderful than we realize.

We both take things one day at a time and are truly grateful for the time God gives us. There is a chance our cancers could return, but we don't live in fear or worry about what might happen.

There have been numerous blessings that have come from this. We gained new compassion for others facing similar situations and we have practical experience to share so they may benefit. We know it's vital to have friends or family to give you a reality check now and then, so you don't wallow in self-pity.

To our fellow spiritual warrior women, know that God's promises are true. He never left us, He never forsook us, and He truly does give peace that surpasses all understanding—the kind that helps you have faith in the face of a devastating diagnosis.

Dear God, thank You for my life and all the blessings You have given. Please help me live each day in gratitude to You. Please give me peace that surpasses all understanding no matter what I may face in days to come. Thank You that Your promises are true. In Jesus' Name, Amen.

God's Promises to Me:

_____

_____

_____

_____

_____

_____

_____

_____

_____

_____

Chapter 37

Walk Through Adversity

with Patti Foster

❧

"Yea, though I walk through the valley of the shadow of death, I will fear no evil; For You are with me; Your rod and Your staff, they comfort me." Psalms 23:4

The unexpected happens. A sudden, catastrophic multi-vehicle traffic crash changed the lives of four women, one man, and their families forever in June of 2002.

At about 6:45 in the evening, and at a temperature of well over 100 degrees, the unexpected happened. Our lives were instantly shattered. Moments before, my three friends from Bible study and I were talking, laughing, and singing, enjoying our fellowship as we drove to our last Bible study meeting before taking a summer break. Now, don't get me wrong. We were definitely not quiet or calm, or anything near this...as most of you can easily imagine!

We were also good, law-abiding citizens with our seat belts securely on. We waited at the red light, enjoying our time, until...

In an instant, our safe and sturdy red Tahoe closed shut like an accordion. We were crushed by tons of metal that barreled down the highway at 70 mph. It did not slow down as it approached the busy, traffic intersection at 6:45 P.M.

The driver had other things on his mind. As he talked on his cell phone, five different drugs coursed through his blood stream as his tractor-trailer rig hauled a load of cars behind him. It mercilessly slammed into us. Lives were forever changed in that instant—including the eyewitnesses and onlookers.

Kind people rushed to the scene, searched for signs of life, and helped. As word of the accident spread, prayers filled Heaven. God was reached by people all over the world. Those at the scene joined hands right then and there and prayed passionately for the crash victims. Doctors and nurses appeared at victims' sides. 9-1-1 was pummeled with emergency calls. Onlookers wondered, *"How could anyone survive such a horrific crash?"* Debris was strewn everywhere. It filled every inch of the intersection.

Thankfully, someone driving a truck noticed a disheveled body in the middle of the left-hand lane of traffic on the north side of the intersection.

It was me.

The shocking sight was my lifeless form. The driver graciously parked his truck in front of my grotesquely ripped-open body, hoping to protect it from oncoming traffic.

As news spread further, family, friends, scores of radio listeners, and other prayer warriors boldly went before God's throne of grace to intercede. *They thanked Him for His faithfulness and mercies to help the families.* And they covered us and the medical teams in continual prayer vigils from different parts of the world.

Fervent persistent prayers from His people together in one accord on behalf of someone or something, reach Almighty God. They move mountains. The impossible is witnessed, and miracles begin!

Corrie Ten Boom put it like this: *"The wonderful thing about praying is that you leave a world of not being able to do something and enter God's realm where everything is possible. He specializes in doing the impossible. Nothing is too great for His almighty power. Nothing is too small for His love."*

When life hangs by a thread and the end seems near, where do you turn? When you can't make sense of what you've seen, heard, or experienced, what do you do? Do you ignore it, pray about it, or try to manipulate things and simply explain it away? Or, perhaps, do you turn to self-destructive behaviors?

When life makes no sense and adversity strikes, true help and guidance only come when we choose to have faith in God— to trust in the Lord with all of our hearts (Proverbs 3:5). We need to cast it ALL onto Him, even the parts that make us mad and

225

hurt. 1 Peter 5:7 tells us to cast "all your cares upon Him, for He cares for you."

You may have guessed by now that, although I was pronounced dead at the scene (I was) and covered with a white sheet (I was), God determined that I should come back to life! (I did!)

But it was not a bed of roses for me, nor was there instantaneous healing. I walked the long and arduous road of traumatic brain injury recovery. Praise be to God, I am still on that journey and it has been difficult, beautiful, and tremendously rewarding.

I had to choose, however. I had to trust God like never before in ways like never before.

When the unexpected happens to you, like it did to me, choose to trust God absolutely. Choose to hold nothing back. When we get honest with God, the Holy Spirit helps us take the next step. It may be only one baby step, but that's enough. *Pour out your heart to God*, all the good and every bit of the bad.

Take a step in His direction. He won't force His way into your heart or pry open the doors you have closed. Yet His tough and tender mercy will draw you. Keep coming toward Him, breath-to-breath, pulse-by-pulse, step-by-step.

Remember that God has a unique way of making good out of bad. Is it easy? Usually not. Does it take much time? More, or sometimes less, than expected.

God has divine plans for using life-twisting hardships. So, whenever you face one, or maybe you're staring at one right now;

226

lay it all in God's hands. Let Him lead you through the times of trouble. Remember Psalms 23:4: "Yea, though I walk through the valley of the shadow of death, I will fear no evil; For You are with me; Your rod and Your staff, they comfort me."

Life affects us. Situations and experiences hurt us. Yet, through it all, the power of prayer moves us on, guiding our decisions and directing our paths. Too often, we allow the "obvious-ness" of our five senses to steal away the blessed assurance of our faith. Prayer meets us where we are and takes us beyond where we can fathom.

When those pesky and uncontrollable "unknowns" flip our worlds upside down, we must not be moved. Give them to Jesus, and then, ask God to help you trust in His control *Let God fight this fight for us. It's His!*

Spiritual warrior women, there is much for us to discover about God's love and care for us. I have learned from my own experience what Corrie ten Boom and her sister, Betsy, learned: that *"no pit is too deep, because God's everlasting arms sustain us."*

When the unexpected happens, stop...drop...and pray. And intimately experience your Shepherd-Lord's deep, deep love that knows no limits—especially as we walk through adversity.

Dear God, thank You that You never leave me—especially when I face difficult times and seasons. Please help me to remember Your faithfulness even through the valley of the shadow of death. Please help me give everything to You and hold nothing back. In Jesus' Name, Amen.

Cares I am Casting on Jesus:

_____

_____

_____

_____

_____

_____

_____

_____

_____

_____

Chapter 38

Stay Grateful Through Grief

with Olga Zapolska

❧

"The Lord is my portion, says my soul, therefore I will hope in Him." Lamentations 3:24, ESV

What is the greater meaning behind tragedy and suffering in our lives? Is the only way to understand life —to walk through death? Can only then we see light in darkness, beauty from ashes, and learn joy in sorrow?

On one dreary March morning, when the city was still asleep, and dawn was struggling to break through heavy rain clouds, my phone suddenly rang. It was a phone call no mother should ever receive. Ever. My son, my first born, was killed by a drunk driver in a horrible crash. My boy was gone because someone had made bad choices. Only 14 hours earlier, my son had called me, his face gleamed with happiness, and despite being 17 years old, he still had an open and candid smile of a child. The only desire in the world I had at that moment was to be with my child—to see him, hug him, take away his pain, protect him, and never again let him go. I wanted to spring into action, run, save, bring him back...but I was powerless. We were 6,000 miles apart.

I couldn't breathe. The pain was so strong, I felt like the blood was going to push through my skin. I felt extremely nauseous. I needed someone I could trust, who knew me and would be able to keep me from falling into the abyss. I slowly crawled out of bed, down to the ice-cold floor onto my bare knees. Without any strength, and with a weak and trembling body, I was searching for the presence of the One in whom I believed with my whole heart. The One who was supposed to have control over everything, to whom I committed my whole life and the life of my child. And now I was attempting to hide under the shadow of His wing until this trial was over. I was unable to think. I simply couldn't come up with the correct algorithm inside my brain to comprehend how this could have happened—to *us*.

This was so much more than I could endure. I whispered: "My Father, if it is possible, let this cup pass from me...it is impossible to survive this." I was falling into the abyss, and with that realization, I was trying with all my might to make my spirit praise the Lord for whom He was. I started to thank God for all the days that our son was with us. That was certainly a struggle. It is easy to lift up your hands and glorify God on Sunday morning, but what are you going to do on Wednesday, when you receive a phone call that your child has been killed? How often we want to pray away every problem, especially tragedy, but those shortsighted prayers short-circuit God's perfect plan. There are seasons and situations we need to simply pray through.

I truly believe we are brought to these deserted places so we can learn to place our complete trust in Him. God is greater than the circumstances that stand in our way. We have to make a choice not to let what has happened to us define us but allow Him to use those events to refine and shape us. We can know our Father deeper and be known by Him more profoundly only in moments of tragedy, suffering, or grief.

There at the funeral home, standing on our knees, holding our boy's lifeless hand, my husband and I prayed: "Father, we are still here. Give us strength to walk through this path, show us the purpose of this tragedy."

I started every morning with praising my Savior and every evening, my husband and I glorified His name for who He was in our life. In moments of weakness and frustration, Father whispered: "Don't be afraid, I am with you! I am your God and I will light the way you have to go and I will hold you by your right hand so that you feel my presence and will not stumble."

Through my experience, I have learned that we must just keep on walking and do these three things:

Rejoice. Even as you walk through the valley of the shadow of death, do not let the enemy steal your joy. Sing a song of hope and a melody of faith. The Joy of the Lord is our fortress!

Pray without ceasing/constantly. Always be "on-line" with God and have an ever-open heart to the Lord's leading. Lean on God all the time, never give up looking to Him for help. Come to Him repeatedly during the day. Talk to Him, cry out to Him, lament. Crying does not change the circumstances, but crying out to the Lord through the circumstances changes who we are.

Be thankful in all circumstances. No matter the circumstances, be thankful! I started to thank God for the 6,425 days that our son was with us, for this priceless gift that Father gave us. When we are thankful, He lifts us up. He lifts us up to where He is. Cultivate a spirit of thankfulness even in the midst of trials and heartaches. The voice of thanksgiving is always louder than the voices of evil. We will hear a voice either way. But whose words are you going to believe? I am going to believe the Word of God!

We must not allow the spirit of ingratitude to harden our hearts and chill our relationship with God. "Sing and make music from your heart to the Lord, always giving thanks to God the Father for everything" (Ephesians 5:19-20, NIV). I knew God was changing the depths of my heart, and He moved me on a different level. Only through intimate prayer time and fasting, Father opened my eyes, changed my heart, healed wounds, and granted wisdom (James 1:5). He put my focus on what I have in

232

my journey through sorrow and tragedy—and it is God Himself. Because "The Lord is my portion...I will put my hope in Him" (Lam. 3:22-24, ESV). There is no greater tragedy in the world for a parent than the death of a child. But He is more than enough for me, or anyone, to continue the race with joy and bring all glory to His Almighty Name.

Dear God, please help me to turn to You and give You thanks and praise at all times in my life, through the good and the unbearable. Help me to truly know that You are my portion and my hope. Please help me to walk with You and trust You day by day. Please be my source of strength and joy. In Jesus' Name, Amen.

I am Grateful to God for:

_____

_____

_____

_____

_____

_____

_____

_____

_____

Chapter 39

Overcome Anxiety

with Rita Halter Thomas

❧

"I sought the Lord, and He heard me, and delivered me from all my fears." Psalms 34:4

I lay frozen in position, flat on my back, fingers laced to cradle my head as I stared at the ceiling. After several minutes, I closed my eyes and tried to sleep, but the machine's loud warble prevented it. I remember drifting once or twice when its rhythm shifted to a steady cadence; still noisy but lulling enough to relax me until the rhythm changed again.

Then it happened. About 40 minutes in, my face flushed with heat and sweat beaded on my upper lip. A whooshing in my ears matched the intensity of my heart rate as it spiked and pounded against my chest. My mind began to race. *What is happening? Am I about to have a heart attack? Will anyone notice something's wrong?* Then I remembered a friend describing what it felt like to have an anxiety attack.

"I'm experiencing some anxiety," I called to the technician running the MRI.

"I need just five more minutes if you can hang with me," came the reply.

"OK," I said, but I'm sure my reply was weak.

Just breathe through it. Deep breath in, and out. In and out. Slowly now. As my heart began to slow, I became aware that my thoughts had shifted. I was singing a hymn. I couldn't string two thoughts together, but my mind defaulted to a song. It was also my prayer. "Jesus, Jesus, Jesus..."

I had never experienced any semblance of a panic or anxiety attack—not like that—not before nor since. If that one experience was a glimpse into the world of those who suffer from a clinical diagnosis of anxiety, they have my greatest empathy. My body's physiological response at that moment was something I do not ever care to experience again.

I won't attempt to address clinical anxiety as I am not a doctor, nor have I ever been diagnosed with anxiety or depression.

But, I have experienced panic. Two specific times come to mind—each involving a choking horse on our mini-ranch. Fortunately, my daughter worked for a veterinarian at the time, knew what to do, and calmly proceeded to do so. My mind raced, my blood pressure rose, but not in the same was as during the MRI.

I also have a long history of self-imposed worry, stress, and anxiety.

I experience more than my share of sleepless nights and too much on my mind. Projects due. Juggling finances. Tight schedules. For me, this type of anxiousness is based on fear. When I say "worry," I don't mean concern, I mean fretting. When I am concerned about something, I'm seeking a solution. Fretting just keeps me balled up inside, unable to think clearly, and probably involves nausea. God tells us in several places in Scripture, "Do not be afraid..."; "Fear not..." or "do not worry." Fear sits at the core of my worry. Fear of failure. Fear of loss. Fear of whatever.

When my husband and I first married 33 years ago, he frequently told me, "you are going to die of a heart attack before you're 30 if you keep this up." He was referring to my stress level. I worried about everything causing stress for both of us. Money. Time. Life. Death. As if that wasn't enough, I worked in print media—a revolving door for daily stress, deadlines, and problem-solving challenges—an environment ripe for growing anxiety.

My sisters, some of you relate. It's a battle sometimes, isn't it? Obviously, I did not die before the age of 30, so something must have changed. It did. I learned how to cope by letting go and giving my concerns and worries to God. I admit, I sometimes still struggle. Camping out in my head, in my own thoughts, can stress me out. The enemy knows this and tries to use it against me. It is a spiritual battle, no doubt.

But when I remember the words of Paul in Philippians 4:6-7: "Be anxious for nothing, but in everything by prayer and supplication, with thanksgiving, let your requests be made known to God; and the peace of God, which surpasses all understanding, will guard your hearts and minds through Christ Jesus." Yes, take it to God and let Him handle it, and do so *daily*.

If we keep reading, we learn from Paul where to place our focus. "Finally, brethren, whatever things are true, whatever things are noble, whatever things are just, whatever things are pure, whatever things are lovely, whatever things are of good report, if there is any virtue and if there is anything praiseworthy—meditate on these things. The things which you learned and received and heard and saw in me, these do, and the God of peace will be with you" (Philippians 4:8-9).

Thinking about good things, pure things, lovely things, and praiseworthy things reminds my head what I know in my heart and that helps me focus on what matters. Then peace settles in my soul because I know God can handle anything. Spiritual warrior women, we can trust Him, even when the answers are not what we want or expect. Even when things go wrong, we can find good in it. Psalms 34:4 is a powerful reminder: "I sought the Lord, and He heard me, and delivered me from all my fears."

I still can't explain why I experienced physical anxiety in an open MRI. Perhaps to relate to those who experience serious anxiety, even if only to understand a little. I had no control over how my body reacted. What I do know is that God knew. He knows everything and cannot be surprised by anything. I know I trust Him. My "default" was to cry out to my Lord in song. Unable to think, I prayed by singing to Jesus and He delivered me.

What is your default or typical response? Do you naturally cry out to Jesus when you're feeling stressed, worried, or anxious?

It is part of life to experience all of those feelings. It is part of life to "walk through the valley of the shadow of death" (Psalms 23:4). Note the word, "through." This means we don't stay there. God brings us out on the other side.

But while we are there sisters, let us pray to take heart and "fear no evil" (Psalms 23:4) because God is with us. Let us continually seek the Lord. He will hear us.

Dear God, when I have stress, worries, and anxiety, please help me call out to You. Let my natural response be turning to You in times of trouble. Please deliver me. In Jesus' Name, Amen.

What the Bible Says About Not Giving in to Fear:

_____

_____

_____

_____

_____

240

Chapter 40

Receive Ultimate Healing

with Autumn Ruark

❦

"But He was wounded for our transgressions, He was bruised for our iniquities; The chastisement for our peace was upon Him, and by His stripes we are healed." Isaiah 53:5

While Jesus was in a certain town, a man came along who was covered with leprosy. When he saw Jesus, he fell with his face to the ground and begged him, "Lord, if you are willing, you can make me clean." Jesus reached out His hand and touched the man. "I am willing," he said. "Be clean!" And immediately the leprosy left him" (Luke 5:12-13, NIV).

For the past three years, I have worked as a nurse in a hospital. I have seen many people who are hurting, both mentally and physically. They are all people who hope someone

241

will have compassion for them and heal or at least treat their diseases.

In my time working closely with patients, I have observed when people are ill and in pain, they tend to become desperate. They are often unaware or have forgotten Jesus still has compassion for them during times of illness. In the moment, God seems far away; the truth is, He is very near.

God remains close to us during our times of heartache and our times of trouble. When the leper cried "Lord, if you are willing, you can make me clean" (Luke 5:12, NIV) our Savior immediately responded, "I am willing; be clean!" (Luke 5:13, NIV). There was no hesitation, no bargaining, and no withholding. What a wonderful reminder that Jesus is willing to heal us and that He cares for our needs! Scripture tells us that right after Jesus told the leper He was willing, "Jesus reached out his hand and touched the man." This may not seem like a critical detail to us now, but in Jesus' day, a person with leprosy was considered unclean and was required to live outside of the city to prevent the disease from spreading. The medical community of that time believed leprosy was spread by human contact, and that it was very contagious. Therefore, lepers were forced to live a very secluded and isolated life. This makes the act of Jesus touching the man and healing him even more powerful, because He knew what the man was needing. Christ, in His wonderful compassion, not only removed the man's leprosy, but laid His hand on him, showing that despite the disease, the isolation, and the loneliness, he was cared for and loved.

The encounter with the leper is just one of many stories throughout the Bible that detail the compassion of Jesus. The woman brought before him to be stoned, who had been caught in the act of adultery; the tax collector Zacchaeus; and the rich young ruler who believed he could earn his way into Heaven—the Lord knew all their thoughts, their sins, their motives, and still chose to love them and show compassion to them.

These examples demonstrate the compassion Jesus has for our physical needs, and they point us to something even more important: our need for a Savior. This is the ultimate healing; it is eternal. Inevitably, our bodies will eventually start to give out, our sight will fade, our knees will hurt, and more. However, our soul lasts forever—either in eternal paradise with Jesus, or in eternal suffering in Hell.

Sin is the ultimate disease. Like the leprosy in Luke Chapter 5, it isolates us—not from others, but from God Himself. Because of sin, we are separated from God and in need of the healing touch of a Savior: "...for all have sinned and fall short of the glory of God." (Romans 3:23, NIV).

The Bible talks extensively about sin as a disease. Sin is a corruption of God's intent for His creation. It is the destruction of what God had intended to be pure. The first humans, Adam and Eve, rebelled against their Maker and listened to the lies of the devil, believing God had cheated them out of something they deserved. This resulted in the fall, and humanity was cursed as a result. Romans 6:23 specifically deals with this condition of man. It gives the diagnosis and prognosis of the disease: "...the wages of sin is death" (NIV).

Death is what we have earned for ourselves because of our sin. It isolates us from the Giver of Life. On our own, in our sinful nature, there is no way to earn back life. However, the rest of the Romans 3:23 provides the cure for the disease: "but the free gift of God is eternal life in Christ Jesus our Lord" (ESV). God knows our disease. In His compassion, He sent His only Son, Jesus, to take upon Himself what we earned and deserve. He did this to make us whole again and bring us back to peace with God. Romans 5:8 says that "God shows His love for us in that while we were still sinners, Christ died for us." We can come to Jesus the same way the leper did: sick, hurting, covered with an incurable disease, isolated, and alone. Jesus responds to us the same way He did to the leper: "I am willing, be clean!" Will you go to Him and receive ultimate healing?

Dear God, thank You for sending Your Son to die in my place. I want ultimate healing. I receive Jesus as my Lord and Savior. Amen.

Areas of My Life Where God is Healing Me:

_____

_____

_____

_____

Going Deeper

Share the Gospel

with JoAnn Doyle

"For I am not ashamed of the Gospel of Christ." Romans 1:16

Suppose one bright sunny day you peered into your mailbox and tucked inside was an exquisitely adored letter, personally addressed to you. As you carefully opened the linen envelope you read a beautifully handwritten note inviting you to the royal palace for an intimate party with the queen. How would you feel? Special and honored to have been invited? How would you reply to the queen's invitation? With a resounding "yes," followed by quickly clearing your calendar and running out to buy the perfect dress?

Well you, beloved daughter of the King, have been given a far more precious, golden-engraved invitation from the Lord Jesus Christ Himself. Personally addressed and hand-delivered to you in Matthew 28. "Who me," you ask? Absolutely!

Jesus' deep & intimate love for you is eternal. His love so all-encompassing He desires none should perish apart from knowing Him, but that all should come to repentance in Him, enjoying the same personal relationship with Jesus as you do.

Because of His vast love and intense desire for all to spend eternity with Him, Jesus has given us, the Body of Christ, the great honor of inviting His most noble guests to the celebration party soon to take place in heaven. He's given each and every one of us invitations to hand out freely to anyone and everyone we meet. Along with specific instructions, Jesus has promised that He will be with us when we tell folks about this once-for-all-eternity celebration.

So why then, do many of us, as followers of Jesus, reject His invitation to "go and make disciples of all nations?" (Matthew 28:19, NIV). Or, perhaps you may have the desire to tell others of the hope within you but shrink back in fear. Perhaps a level of uncertainty or lack of confidence in sharing our faith is involved. But often, I'm sad to say, we back down out of fear of being ridiculed or rejected.

Paul's words in Romans 1:16 convict my heart and propel me with renewed holy boldness when he confidently says, "For I am not ashamed of the Gospel of Christ" (NKJV). Ouch, that's the convicting part. Paul is not ashamed of Jesus— and we shouldn't be either! He goes on to say, "for it is the power of God to salvation for everyone who believes." This is the part that can propel you into holy boldness too! When we bravely open our mouths telling of the love and goodness of God in His Son Jesus, God's power is released into the other person's life. The Holy Spirit begins drawing them to the Father. God's Word begins accomplishing what He desires, not returning to Him empty. These are not just nice-sounding words, sisters. These are promises from God's Word.

If fear, uncertainty, or doubt is your companion when it comes to sharing the Good News of Jesus Christ, you're in good company. The disciples struggled with the same insecurities, even after spending three and a half years with Jesus. Leading up to Jesus' Great Commission invitation, all but one of them fled during His most trying hours of life, as He hung dying on the cross. It was the women and John, who remained faithfully at His side.

Three days later, the hiding men, nursed their despair, doubt and fear, while the faith-filled women bravely set out to anoint Jesus' precious body. Those courageous women were given the greatest of gifts when they discovered Jesus was ALIVE, running back to the men with the message of good news of great joy that Jesus was no longer dead but risen from the grave! The reverberation of this eternal message continues to ring loud and clear. Today, we often see a similar pattern, women in various cultures are often the first to learn the astounding truth that Jesus is alive then bring the Good News back to their men.

I want to be a part of the movement of women brave enough to lead the way, don't you? It all begins with holy boldness in living out the Word of God! In Matthew 28, we find the disciples gazing intently at resurrected Jesus. Their first action was to worship Him. Worship is always the perfect response.

When Isaiah saw the Lord seated on a throne, high and lifted up, the train of His robe filling the temple, he was undone as he entered the holy worship of Heaven. When vast armies came against Jehoshaphat and the children of Israel in 2 Chronicles 20:15, the king cried out to God for deliverance, "We have no power against this vast army that is attacking us. We do not know what to do, but our eyes are on You" (NIV). God answered, "Do not be afraid...for the battle is not yours, but [Mine]." Jehoshaphat and all of Judah fell with their faces to the ground and worshiped the Lord. Worship is always the perfect response!

The disciples nailed it with their worship! But they blew it with their emotional response of doubt, for mixed in with their worship was wavering faith.

In Scripture, when an angel was sent from God, fear was the usual response. The angel would say: "do not be afraid." Whether it was Sarah in the Old Testament, or Mary in the New Testament, neither were reprimanded for being afraid.

Fear is one thing, but doubt is another matter entirely. Doubt is not a virtue, nor is it humility. When Peter walked on water beside Jesus, it was doubt that caused him to sink. Jesus did not commend him for it, He rebuked Peter, just as He did the eleven when they doubted Jesus in His resurrected appearing. Doubt is a distraction from truth. Doubt is convenient because it excuses us from having to act. Bottom line, doubt is unbelief and unbelief is sin! Jesus is calling us to get past it, not embrace it.

Our merciful God remembers we are but dust and makes provision for our human frailties. We can cry out with the father in Mark 9:24, whose son was delivered of demons, "Lord, I believe; help my unbelief" (NKJV). And He will answer, just as He did the eleven, He cherished so dearly.

Two thousand years ago, Jesus promised His disciples that His all-surpassing power would go with them when they told others the Good News. The same power our Triune God used at Earth's creation is the power Jesus entrusts to us. That power parted the Red Sea, fed manna to the children of Israel and raised Jesus from the dead. It has not been diluted, lessened, or weakened by time. And it's the exact same power Jesus imparts to His followers today.

Jesus put the disciples' and our fears to rest when He said, "And be sure of this: I am with you always, even to the end of the age" (Matthew 28:20, NLT). How comforting is that?! Every time we share the Gospel, Jesus is at our side, cheering us on. The Holy Spirit within, providing divine direction.

Chile's Atacama Desert is the driest desert in the world. It holds the record for the world's longest dry streak, having gone 173 months without a single drop of rain. This desert is so arid it's often used as a stand-in for Mars, both in films and by NASA for rover experiments. In 2015, a storm brought in .96 inches of rain in a single day. Though this seems like a minuscule amount of moisture, it accounted for over 14 years' worth of rain in one day. The result was a spectacular 600-mile carpeted display of breathtakingly beautiful flowers. For years, countless tiny flower seeds laid dormant under the dry desert floor. All they needed was a tiny drop of life-giving water and abundant sunshine to sprout and flourish in new life.*

The same can be said for many people we meet who are spiritually parched, thirsting for truth. We have the Living Water they long for. When we step out with holy boldness and share the love of Jesus, they may spring to new life like the Atacama Desert.

Shireen is a 70-ish Syrian refugee who carried the weight of the world on her thin shoulders. Her home was destroyed and loved ones still trapped in her home city. Shireen was desperate without hope. When I met this dear woman, I listened to her story and felt her pain. I asked if I could tell her a story from God's Word. As I told her the story of Jesus, in the boat with His twelve closest friends when He calmed the storm, she sat forward eagerly listening. Shireen told me she could understand the fear of Jesus' friends, and that she, too, had many storms in her life. I asked if she would like to hear another true story from the Word of God, for we know the life-giving power in Scripture.

I then told Shireen my story, how I tried to reach God though my religion. But how keeping rules and praying rote prayers didn't make me feel any closer to God. I explained that my whole life changed when I understood what the Bible taught; that Jesus loved me and died in my place to remove my sins. How Jesus was calling me into a relationship with Him. It wasn't about keeping rules, but believing Jesus was God's Son, raised from the dead. My part was to believe and ask Jesus to forgive me and receive His gift of eternal life. When I prayed to Jesus, recognizing these truths, I told Shireen, the emptiness in my heart was finally filled with complete peace and love and I had assurance I would spend eternity in heaven with Jesus, when I took my final breath on earth.

Shireen beamed as she listened, asking how she could have that peace too, for she was also empty inside with no hope for heaven. With tears streaming down her tanned cheeks, Shireen gloriously gave her life to the One who loves her most.

You see, sisters, the power is in God's Word. We may not get to the place where a person we're sharing with is ready to pray. That's okay. Our part is to share the Gospel, it's God's place to bring them to salvation.

When we put our confidence in God's Word, not our own words, fear and doubt flee. When you're in the moment, pause and pray, asking the Lord to give you His thoughts and words. Remember how blessed we are to carry Jesus to a lost and dying world.

Our beloved Savior has given us this beautiful invitation to be a part of rescuing lost souls. How are you going to RSVP? Like Paul, we can confidently say, "I am not ashamed of the Gospel of Christ!" and step out in faith with each divine encounter the Lord provides.

Then watch... God work... as only He can.

* https://www.cntraveler.com/stories/2015-10-30/chile-atacama-desert-is-now-a-floral-wonderland

Part 3

The Sisterhood
of
Prayer Warriors

About the Author

Dr. Angela Ruark

Dr. Angela Ruark is a writer, adjunct professor, and long-time math and science teacher. She is an author in several award-winning math textbooks and the editor of *The Lens of East Texas*, an online Christian news outlet. She also holds a bachelor's degree in mathematics and a master's degree in science education (chemistry).

Angela is the founder of *A 180 Degree Turn*, an organization that promotes God's principles for education. She recently partnered with Stand Firm Ministries as general editor for the award-winning devotional, *Invincible*.

Angela lives in Texas with her husband, Bill, of twenty-nine years. They have three wonderful sons. Her hobbies include languages, beekeeping, and the occasional cliff jumping.

Contact Angela at facebook.com/drangelaruark and @drangelaruark

Contributing Writers

Amanda Mc Candless

Amanda McCandless is a mother, an early childhood educator focused on behavioral management, and pastor's wife. She is a graduate of Central Baptist College and the University of Central Arkansas with a degree in early childhood education.

After spending several years at home with her two daughters, Andrea and Addison, Amanda now teaches upper elementary ALE (Alternative Learning Education for students who struggle with classroom behavior). Her goal has been to follow wherever the Lord leads. This has led Amanda to becoming a life-long student of prayer and over 20 years of ministry with her husband, Jake.

Pat Self

Pat Self is the founder of Bride of Life International Ministries. She describes herself as a Connecticut Yankee but lover of Texas, a place she now calls home. Pat provides biblical counseling and outreach for her local community and across the country. Her Facebook live ministry program offers Bible lessons, prayers, discussion of current events, and interviews with ministry and community leaders. You can find Pat on Facebook at facebook.com/BrideofLife or at https://milee4831.wixsite.com/brideoflife. If you see her in person, be sure she gives you one of her signature "Hug Passes."

262

Misha Goetz

Growing up as the only child to modern day psalmist Marty Goetz and his wife Jennifer. Misha says, "As a Messianic Jew, my dream is to unite Christian and Jew in worship of the Holy One of Israel". Her style of worship builds upon decades of her father's ministry and yet incorporates her own youthful style and anointing.

Misha lives Nashville with her husband Joshua Hoyt, and their son, Caleb Vincent Hoyt. She travels the country leading worship full-time. Her latest release is a DVD with her father Marty Goetz, filmed LIVE overlooking Jerusalem with a 26-piece orchestra. This and more available at itsmishamusic.com

Shelly Wilson

Shelly Wilson is a modern-day psalmist, writer, and poet. Her passion is in mentoring and counseling women to become all Christ designed them to be. Her latest book is *From the Meadow's Ledge.* You will find Shelly listening intently to hearts in support groups and meetings where dreaming big is a way of life with Jesus. She oversees the publishing of a Christian magazine for girls and a new online digital women's magazine that is dedicated to providing an opportunity for women to share their music, art, and writing with others. You can learn more about the ministries Shelly is involved with at www.shellywilsonministries.org.

Dana Crosby

Dana holds a bachelor's degree from the University of Michigan, a master's degree from the Assemblies of God Theological Seminary, and has traveled the world preaching and teaching the Word of God. Her mission is to help others understand the Bible better so they can have a better relationship with God.

She is the creator of the wildly popular YouTube Series "What Your Pastor Never Told You About the Book of Revelation" for the Wisdom Calls Channel, and her website: www.WhatYourPastorNeverToldYou.com. She has numerous free teaching materials available online including her End Times Masterclass. Dana is married to her husband Jonathan and they have three children: Emma, Maximus, and True.

Beckie Lindsey

Beckie Lindsey is an award-winning author of the *Beauties from Ashes* series, poet, blogger, and the editor of *Southern California Christian Voice,* a division of *One Christian Voice,* a national news syndicating agency. She is a major coffeeholic and enjoys a good book with a cat on her lap. She also loves to hike and hang out with family and friends. Beckie and her husband, Scott have three adult children, two adorable cats and live in California.

Tamikia Bell

Tamikia Bell (Tami) is a licensed chemical dependency counselor, anger resolution therapist, and founder of Bell's Mentoring & Counseling Center. She focuses on using biblical principles to renew a person's thought process throughout recovery.

Tami is the author of *The Stewardship of Parenting: A Priceless Investment*. She has served as a youth minister, intercessory prayer minister, an associate pastor, and over five years as a prison counselor. Her insights into recovery and parenting transcend national and ethnic boundaries, denominational barriers, and reach beyond intellect to touch the heart.

Tami and her husband, Greg, have seven children. Look for her upcoming podcast, "How You Think About What You Think About," available at bmacc.net.

Tracy Malone

Tracy Malone is a Registered Nurse Case Manager, homeschool expert, and has been married to Mike for 40 years. They have lived all over Texas while raising their four sons ages 17 to 40. They now enjoy eight grandchildren ages five and a half to almost 16. Together, they thank the Lord for their sons, who are a blessing in their lives and in the lives of those they touch. Tracy and Mike are blessed to serve the Lord, their community, and their church. Their hearts' desire is that the work of their hands brings glory to God.

265

Becky Wangner

Becky Wangner and husband, Rob, have been married for 22 years. They have adopted 4 children from Russian orphanages. (All now grown). Becky worked in video and radio production for many years, as well as coordinating Christian conferences.

In recent years, Becky has organized numerous End-Time and missions conferences around the country, featuring international speakers. Becky has a passion for biblical archaeology and has taken a number of trips to explore biblical sites.

Carrie Gill

Carrie Gill is a wife, mother, and grandmother. She has been married to husband, Rocky, for 29 years. They have two daughters, a son-in-law, a granddaughter, and another on the way.

Carrie attended Baylor University and taught elementary school for several years. When her first child was born, she changed careers to be a stay-at-home-mom. Carrie loves to read, spend time with her granddaughter, play games with friends, and piddle around in the yard. Carrie and Rocky are native Texans and reside in East Texas, along with three dogs and two cats.

Caroline George

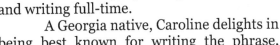

Caroline George is a multi-award-winning author of YA speculative fiction. (Her latest book *Dearest Josephine* releases from Thomas Nelson, Harper Collins February 2021.) She graduated from Belmont University with a degree in publishing and public relations, and now travels the country, speaking at conferences and writing full-time.

A Georgia native, Caroline delights in being best known for writing the phrase, "Coffee first. Save the world later." When she's not glued to her laptop, she can be found hiking in the Appalachian Mountains, sipping a lavender latte, or chatting with young writers. Find her on Instagram @authorcarolinegeorge and Twitter @CarolineGeorge.

Heather Stoner

Heather Stoner came to Texas by way of Connecticut and Virginia. Texas was the birthplace of her father and has been the place God called her to carry on his legacy. She is blessed to be raised by parents that set an example of serving the Lord daily.

Years of being a home school mom, working in human resources and being involved with nonprofits and politics gives Heather many opportunities to work on grace and be in need of God's grace. She is the mother of her darling daughter, who lives in Washington, D.C. and to Lilly the Westie. Connect with Heather on Facebook at the Winsome Cottage Writings Blog.

Bunni Pounds

Bunni Pounds is the president and founder of Christians Engaged, a nonprofit organization dedicated to motivating Christians to pray for their nation, vote, and engage the culture. She and her husband, Tim, have been bi-vocational and active in Christian ministry for over twenty years. Bunni is a Bible teacher, public speaker, author, songwriter, and led worship for many years.

She has a Bachelor of Arts & Sciences degree in Political Science from Dallas Baptist University and an associate degree in Theology from Christ for the Nations Institute in Dallas. Bunni and Tim have been married for twenty-three years and have two sons, Israel and Ben, and two daughters-in-law, Teodora and Giulia.

Sheryl Coffey

Sheryl Coffey is the founder of The Fragrant Hours Ministry. She and her husband, Lee, have been in ministry for more than 25 years. Sheryl often speaks to women's groups and shares her story using a collection of perfume bottles to illustrate biblical lessons from the making of perfume.

Her story has been featured on Joni and Friends and various television programs. Sheryl has been published in several Christian publications. She also serves as the President/CEO of a non-profit in East Texas, where she and Lee make their home. Connect with Sheryl at thefragranthours.org

Nicole Fitzpatrick

Nicole and her husband, Jason, work among the poor, marginalized descendants of the Aztec Indians. Their ministry has resulted in many house churches throughout south central Mexico over the past 29 years, often in remote villages where Christ had never been preached.

In 2004, Nicole answered her heart's call and began taking in abandoned, abused, and orphaned children, many of whom are trafficking victims. She and Jason started The Village Children's Home. They welcome any child rescued, homeless, or at risk. Ten years ago, Nicole and Jason began opening Drug Rehabs and serve hundreds of youth and men. Find out more at www.thevillageglobal.com.mx

Dr. Grace English

Grace C. English, M.D. is a practicing board-certified Internal Medicine physician, founder of CARE (Christ-centered Abortion Recovery & Education) & co-founder of Bethesda Health Clinic (for working uninsured adults) with her husband John P. English, M.D.

Dr. English holds a bachelor's degree from the University of Texas at Austin. She earned her medical degree from the University of Texas Southwestern Medical School and completed her residency at Presbyterian Hospital in Dallas. Grace and John are proud parents of their three adult children Sarah, Daniel and Matthew. They are actively involved in their Church, community and faith-based organizations.

Rita Halter Thomas

✴

Rita Halter Thomas is an award-winning writer, author, and former newspaper and magazine publisher. She recently co-authored the award-winning devotional, *Invincible*, with Stand Firm Ministries founder Jake McCandless.

Rita is a member of the Blue Ridge Mountain Christian Writers Conference, staff writer and editor for Stand Firm Ministries, founder of www.thewriteeditor.com, and editor of MidArk Christian Voice. She is also a pastor's wife and mother.

Rita enjoys assisting aspiring authors by using the combined skills from her years in media publishing with her experience in Christian book publishing. She also enjoys spending time with her family, serving her church, and horseback riding. Find Rita at www.thewriteeditor.com.

Linda Dill

✴

Linda Dill is a pastor's wife, mother, grandmother, and great-grandmother. She serves as treasurer and board member for Shepherd's Heart Ministry. Linda and her husband, Dr. James Dill, have been in ministry for over 60 years and have lived in California, Canada, Hawaii, and Texas. You can connect with Linda at www.theshepherdsheart.org.

Susan Ellsworth

Susan Ellsworth was born to Dr. James and Linda Dill in Salinas, California. She moved with her family to Texas in the mid 1970s. Susan attended Lee College in Cleveland, Tennessee. She moved back to Texas and pursued her nursing degree. She has been an RN for 26 years. Susan also serves on the Board of Directors for a local charter school. She has been married to her husband, Les, for 31 years, and they have three adult children.

Patti Foster

Patti Foster was a media personality and voice-over talent in different parts of the United States...until she horrifically suffered a severe traumatic brain injury in a fatal traffic crash. After being considered dead on a hot Texas highway, Patti leans into life and lays hold of each moment, as she perseveres through adversity.

She has learned, firsthand, that Hope appears on the scene in all shapes and sizes. It has no limits...knows no boundaries. Patti travels around the world speaking and offering hope to anyone dealing with trouble. Visit Patti at: www.pattifoster.com or email her at: patti@pattifoster.com

Olga Zapolska

Olga Zapolska works in the wealth management industry and is a writer and speaker. She obtained her master's degrees in Science of Engineering and in Business Administration. Olga speaks at Christian retreats, women's conferences, and for MADD (Mothers Against Drunk Driving). She and her husband lead the Grief Share Program that helps people move from mourning to joy through focusing on God's Word and sharing their experiences. Olga and her husband, Leonard of 23 years, have four fabulous children. Pasha (in Heaven), Zakhar 16, Solomon 10, Anna 9. They reside in Texas and love to travel around the world.

Autumn Ruark

Autumn Ruark is a registered nurse and graduate of the University of Texas at Tyler in 2016. She was inducted into the Sigma Theta Tau International Honor Society of Nursing before graduating and started her career. Her career began at CHRISTUS Trinity Mother Frances Hospital on a medical surgical unit, during which time she achieved her Certified Medical Surgical Nurse certificate. She then transferred to an outpatient surgical center. Autumn has been married for four and a half years to her husband, Paul, a singer, songwriter, and musician. Autumn has had the opportunity to co-write and sing on some of his Christian songs. Her hobbies include art, cooking, decorating, traveling, and exercise.

JoAnn Doyle

JoAnn Doyle and husband, Tom, of 40 years, have 6 children and 10 grandchildren. JoAnn was a pastor's wife for 20 years prior to full-time mission work in the Middle East. She founded *Not Forgotten*, which ministers Christ's love to Jewish and Muslim women throughout the Middle East and U.S. In 2017, God called the Doyles to begin *Uncharted Ministries*, inspiring believers to join God's harvest among Jews and Muslims.

JoAnn appears on national TV and radio programs including John Ankerberg, Focus on the Family, Moody Radio with Chris Fabry, and Charlie Dyer and Mission Network News.

She and Tom co-authored *Women Who Risk, Secret Agents for Jesus in the Muslim World,* and *Breakthrough-The Return of Hope to the Middle East.* Worship and prayer are the heart of JoAnn's life along with a deep love for her family.
Learn more at: UnchartedMinistries.com/NotForgotten
and I foundthetruth.com.

Cover Artist: Emily McLean

Emily McLean is a graphic designer and animator from Wheeling, West Virginia. She obtained her degree in Digital Media and Design from West Liberty University. She spends most of her days painting or creating new pieces. In her work she enjoys combining hand painted art with digital and draws her inspiration from the beauty of nature.

GO BEYOND THE 40 DAYS,
JOIN THE

SORORITY
OF
SPIRITUAL WARRIORS

Join Now

Spiritual Warrior Woman
40-Day Devotional
Vol. 2

COMING
MAY 2021

SIGN-UP FOR ALERTS

WWW.SPIRITUALWARRIORWOMANPRAY.COM

IF YOU ENJOYED THIS DEVOTIONAL, THEN YOU WILL LIKE <u>INVINCIBLE</u>.

A STAND FIRM BOOK'S DEVOTIONAL,
AWARD WINNING,
EDITED BY DR. ANGELA RUARK,
CO-AUTHORED BY RITA HALTER THOMAS.

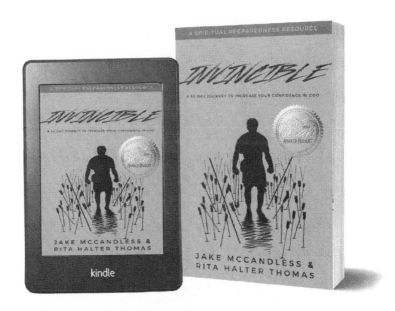

AVAILABLE NOW

GET YOUR COPY AT
WWW.STANDFIRMBOOKS.COM/INVINCIBLE

IF YOU ENJOYED THIS DEVOTIONAL, THERE'S ONE FOR MEN, TOO.

COMING SOON